Did I J[...]

Poe[...]ree of Life

Short Stories, Dreams, Visions, Poems and Plays written by
Joseph Taliaferro aka Brother P

I Would Like to Thank Yahshua, My Wife and children, My Parents , the rest of my Family and friends for all the support love and encouragement that they have given me throughout the years

Table of contents

In this life

In this life I never wanted to be alone

in this life I wanted someone to call my own

In this life looking for love in so many places

in this life I thought I found love in too many faces

in this life never give up even when you get weary

Jesus heal a broken heart if you are lonely I pray you can hear me

we all need someone who cares

someone to share

someone to hold

in a world that sometimes cold

we need someone to love

someone to hug

we need someone that's real

who knows exactly how we Feel

There's a void that is deep inside

you can run but you cannot hide

the choice is yours do you want to ride

we slip and slide repent and then we bounce back, there is a cost that we must pay did you count that ,love is a process we headed for perfection glorified bodies in the spirit that's his selection, I needed love and made some big mistakes to all the ladies that I loved forgive me no hate ,I apologize I had to realize when love cries a dove flies as tears drop eyes begin to see clearly, Jesus Loves you I pray that you can hear me

Joseph Taliaferro bka Brother P

Footprints in the dirt

While enjoying my lemonade, I remember being in the house one Good Friday getting ready for a party. I had invited several of my best friends over because we partied every weekend. Harry and Jack would always come over first. Harry was into cards, poker and spades, but tarot was his specialty. Jack—now he was crazy. He carried a colt 45 everywhere he went. Mary and Jezebel joined us later and that's when the high times would begin. My frat brother Osiris was always on the scene, too. His knowledge ran deep. Once we all gathered together, there was no telling what would happen. Usually when Jack started yelling, Mary would hightail it out of there. She was into chilling. But once Jack calmed down, then ,a few hours later, Mary would come right back.

This Good Friday, there was a knock at the door around 5:30 pm. I had no idea who in the world it could be since all my friends had arrived. Harry told me not to open the door because it could be a Mormon or a Jehovah's Witness. I cracked the door a little and asked the man who was he. He said His name was Yesu, I then asked what He wanted? He replied that He wanted to come in and that He'd been knocking at the door for a long time. I told Him that I had company who did not like strangers but that I would come outside and talk to Him.

While outside we began to walk together down the dirt roads of Carolina. He knew everything about me and it was as though I knew Him, too. He then began to tell me that my friends were not my friends at all. In fact, He said they were trying to kill me. I was shocked at first and proceeded to tell Him that we had been together for so long and were now attached.

In fact, for the most part I had grown to love them. But then He began to show me that Jack was the reason my liver was not healthy. Mary had caused my lungs to become as black as charcoal. Then He revealed that Harry was into divination, a form of witchcraft. And finally, He Showed me that Osiris was really a part of a secret religion that communicated with the dead. I asked, "How do I get rid of them? He said all I had to do was invite Him in and He would handle the rest. And that's when Yesu began to shine real bright.

At first, I could not even look at Him. Then He said, "Yes, I am the God of your youth." He went on and said that my body would become the temple of the Holy Spirit. I just fell to my knees and began to repent and ask for forgiveness. When I stood up we began to walk back to my house. Somehow, it was now Saturday morning and I stood on my back porch looking at the dirt road. I noticed that there was only one set of footprints in the dirt. I said to myself that I was dreaming. And that's when a voice came out of nowhere and said that it was not a dream. The voice said, "When you repented and believed on me as the Son of the Living God, I entered your heart. That's why you only see one set of footprints. No longer was I outside walking beside you, knocking at the door of your heart.

I was now inside. Once you invited me in, I kicked Harry, Mary, Jack, and Jezebel out." I then wanted to know why he said his name was Yezu when I answered the door. He replied, "That is my Swahili name. My Hebrew name is Yahshua, but most of you Americans call me Jesus. I went inside the house, I blew the dust off my bible and began to study the Word.

The Impressionable Years

My earliest memories of Yahshua are Sunday at my Big Momma's house waking up to gospel playing on the radio early in the morning. At seven or eight I remember memorizing my first and only Bible verse:

Let not your heart be troubled: you believe in God also in me. In my Father's house are many mansions: if it were not so, I would have told you. I go to prepare a place for you. And if I go to prepare a place for you, I will come again and receive you unto myself; that where I am, you may be also. And where I go you know and the way you know. {John 14: 1-4}

Throughout my first 35 years I can look back now and remember this Bible verse that I had committed to memory at vacation bible school in Moreno Valley California popping into my thoughts at the weirdest times. But even then, the seed was planted in me as a boy and since my youth, I've known who Jesus was—and is.

I am the way truth and the life; no man comes to the Father but by Me. {John 14:6}

Thanks to my parents, my sister and I learned to do the usual Christian traditions growing up, such as going to Sunday School and praying before bed and meals but there was no Bible study at home. We had a Bible in the living room, but it was just there, collecting dust. Yet the Seed of God's word was inside of me and though I had yet to know Him on a personal level, He was still personally involved with me. I can remember one day riding my bike and hitting the front brakes so hard that I went over the front handle bars and landed head first on the street. My head should have been split in two, but I jumped up and ran inside the house with no injuries. I know He was with me.

For he shall give his angels charge over thee, to keep thee in all thy ways. They shall bear thee up in their hands, lest thou dash thy foot against a stone. {Psalms 91: 11&12}

At 18 years of age I went off to college where I was introduced to other religions, philosophies and secret societies. The chaplain of my college not only taught the World Religions class, he was also a member of one of the oldest black fraternities founded in America, Alpha Phi Alpha. Learning so much on the streets and in the classroom about different faiths really challenged my beliefs. This, mixed with living a wild party lifestyle of sex, drugs and hip-hop music, led to much confusion. Now that I was 25 years old I wanted to know what the truth was. So, I went to the public library and started with the Jewish Encyclopedia. That is where I discovered esoteric mysticism called kabbalah. My family pastor had no idea what I was talking about when I questioned him about kabbalah.

It was during this same period I even began reading books by Elijah Muhammad, founder of the Nation of Islam. After writing several short stories and plays, I decided to publish them. I went to a bookstore in Hampton, Virginia and met a man by the name of Khalid Khalifah. He allowed me to print and bind my manuscripts in his office. I would pay him 5 dollars and sell them for 10. One of my plays was about Nat Turner a slave who led a revolt back in the 1800s. Khalid Khalifah also had written a book about Nat Turner, which I found very intriguing. In return for my videotaping his Nat Turner Tour since I was an audio-visual tech, Mr. Khalifah paid me in books.

My first payment was The Message to the Blackman by The Honorable Elijah Muhammad. Now I had already formed somewhat of an opinion of Minister Elijah Muhammed because I had already read Malcolm X's autobiography. But I had never read Elijah Muhammad's book called The Message to the Blackman and the Theology of Time. The books that I read made me doubt who Jesus was. And whatever anger that was in me from growing up in a very racist America, these books were like gasoline that made that small flame grow more.

After working at Hampton University for two years, I decided to move to Newark NJ. Because of my training in audio/video technology, I picked up a job easily at New Jersey Institute of Technology. I was still trying to break into the rap industry as an artist or a producer and finally put an ad in Rap Sheet, a popular hip hop newspaper.

One day while I was waiting in the bank to cash a check, I met a brother by the name of Abdul Hassan. We started talking because I had on my frat jacket. As we talked, I learned he'd danced with one of my frat brothers named Hot Dog, whom I had met on a past rap collaboration project. Abdul Hassan invited me to participate in a video shoot that featured his brother Vid and The Fugees, then an unknown group. We started shooting deep inside the projects of Brick City at 9:30 pm and finished the next morning, often free styling around a trash fire during breaks. I met Abdul and the Fugees again a couple years later at Hampton University. We were backstage at his concert in Ogden hall. I know people must have thought we were crazy as we battle rapped in the basement. I found out later that Wyclef was Haitian. Somehow, I knew that one day we would meet again, and I would greet him in Creole.

Finally, a music manager called me from Los Angeles about the ad in Rap Sheet. He was also a member of my fraternity and I decided to go to Hollywood to pursue my dream. I caught a Greyhound across the country, a wild three-day adventure that ended at the terminal in East LA. Dwayne Cooper, One of my best friends from HU, picked me up and it was on and popping from that point forward.

Even though I was pursuing my music goal at this time, for some reason I began studying even harder to find out what the truth was. My next move consisted of joining Mosque 27 under the Leadership of Minister Tony Muhammed in Los Angeles. Minister Tony was also a member of Omega Psi Phi. I signed up with the Nation of Islam, while recording with Sam Sneed of Death Row records. I was only doing a skit and some background stuff, but it was still my connection to the hip-hop industry. I did not turn that lose, even while searching for the meaning of life.

As I transitioned into the professional hip-hop world, I found myself in Compton, learning how to make my drum tracks better from Anthony Soup Holmes, who was excellent with music production. He was a character, often standing outside his studio to look for UFOs. I never saw any, but he did. I also met Dr. Dre and Snoop, and we did a video with Sam Sneed called Lady Heroin.

While all this was going on my manager introduced me to a lady that was a witch. I recall my manager used her as an accounting consultant, which is how I was introduced to her. She had a big black cat with human-like eyes that was walking around like it owned the place. She spoke of her days in a coven and after a couple of stories I asked why she gave up the craft. She said that one day her coven rose up a demon and could not send it back. Whoa, I thought. Then she told us that while being tormented by a demon she yelled out the name of Jesus. Well, that was confusing, so I asked, "Why would a witch use the name of Jesus?". She told me, "There's power in the name of Jesus." This was the last place I thought I would be hearing about the power in the name of Jesus.

Most of us are familiar with the circumstances surrounding this event: JESUS WEPT and probably the people present on the scene thought that the Master wept because it was too late, he didn't get THERE on TIME to heal his friend who was sick… unaware that they were about to witness the IMPOSSIBLE: LAZARUS come OUT! Jesus has the same power today to resurrect every dead situation and bring our dream to pass!

One day while walking down Hollywood Blvd I came across a Ron Hubbard museum. I knew that he had written a book called Dianetics. My mom had a copy in the house when I was young. I never read it, but I thought the cover was cool. The Cover was a Beautiful Volcano. AS I went inside there were all kinds of artwork of Ron Hubbard's accomplishments on the walls. A host came to me after 20 minutes or so and asked if I would like to see a film. I agreed and sat in a little theatre. After the film the screen rolled up and a volcano model blew up like a giant middle school science project. They then told me about the church and gave me directions. I parked outside of a large building. When I went inside people were walking in all directions. I went to a counter and a lady approached with several books and a cigarette in her mouth. Smoking in a church? I asked her about the books and she began to tell me that this was finance and this one was accounting and then she went about her business. I turned around went out the door and took off in my 1984 Toyota Tercel. That was the Church of Scientology.

My most memorable time during this period in my life was when I performed at The Hollywood Athletics Club, not because of what I did as a poet but because I met Tupac. When he walked by I thought I'd seen a ghost. I was under the impression that he was still in jail. The coolest and strangest show I performed was during a Meshell Ndegeocello showcase. That was the first time I did my hard-core Nat Turner piece in front of so many white folks, and I was surprised they enjoyed it. A week after Tupac got out of jail I totaled my car on Crenshaw Blvd. I remember looking at the car and HEARING a voice say that" **this was my omen to get off the West Coast**." That was a week after I signed up to join Mosque 27 of the Nation of Islam under the leadership of Minister Tony Mohammed. As a side note years later, Minister Tony Muhammed would end up connecting with The Church of Scientology.

Deeper into the Search for the Truth I came back to the East Coast and landed in Hardeeville, SC where I created my own record label, Cross Da Traxxx Entertainment, with two young men from the area, DJ Smoove and MJ.

Cross Da Traxxx Entertainment

When I left the west coast, I ended up in Ft Lauderdale Fla. working as a Bouncer at a Popular beach club. After a month I decided to go back where my mom was born and raised, Hardeeville S.C. My cousin Michael picked me up from the train station in Savannah Ga. Javon Bush my baby cousin picked me up and drove me straight to DJ Smoove's House. And that was the Beginning of Cross Da Traxxx Entertainment.

Letell, DJ Smoove, was still in high school and I was 30 years old. At first things were slow because we were on two different wave lengths. To clarify I was not smoking weed at the time. 6 years earlier I had quit and dabbled a little bit with Christian rap after leaving the west coast. But one day I smoked a Blunt with my DJ and things began to flow like water. In 2 years we would produce 7 complete CDeez.

After our 3 CD we decided to do a concert at the 170 club in Levy. I got off work in Hilton Head and headed to the club. When I got there, everybody was in a room drinking and smoking. The Back Room was packed with all our artist and Cross da Traxxx Associates. There was a nice turnout and we were in the back getting tuned up. In the middle of smoking and drinking John John says let's Pray. The whole room froze. The prayer went forth and we went right back to getting tuned UP.

We took the stage on fire Literally. Everything was on auto pilot. Without any rehearsal we banged the show all the way out. We took a loss on the door because we did not have our people collecting the cash. But that's the Business. We took the little money we made and put it right back into the business.

Back in the Lab we produced Cross da Traxxx volume 4 .and pushed our fan base out to Bluffton SC. We continued to work and in the middle of making Cross Da Traxxx vol. 5. I got a call to come to the dog pound. The dog pound was an actual trap house that also housed our recording equipment. It was very late and in the studio, was a young lady who went by the name of Redrum. They wanted me to test her. We went back and forth rhyme for rhyme song for song poem for poem. Brother P had met his match. She did two songs on the CD and now we were pushing our music to Hilton Head. We also drove down highway 321 stopping in every town to promote our latest CD. We stopped in Estill and found out they also had a Cross da Traxxx .

The Time had come to do another show. This time we worked out the contract so that we would get paid properly. The only problem was security. We informed them that people were coming from all over because of our promotion. Ridgeland, Bluffton, Hilton Head, Levy and Hardeeville in the same place requires good security. They insisted on using their guys.

Before the show a shootout took place in the parking lot. And that was that. Back to the Lab. We would crank out two more projects. One day while recording and smoking a young man ,JR, came in the studio and told me and Smoove the reason why couldn't get anything done. He said we were always smoking. The Bottom line is he was right.

While in Savannah, GA, which was just a few minutes outside of Hardeeville. I stumbled across a bookstore that had the most interesting knowledge I had ever studied up until this point in my life. One of the guys in the book store gave me a book called the Holy Tablets and I read it from cover to cover. I shared the information with a young man selling Nation of Islam newspapers and he got so angry. It was like I had slapped his momma. The knowledge that I had come across was the teachings of Dr. Malachi Z. York. This man had answers for everything; in fact, his organization had a fraternal element to it. They claimed their knowledge was the real stuff.

It was so weird that everyone had some type of affiliation with the Freemasons. Elijah Muhammad was a freemason. His book, The Secrets of Freemasonry, is an eye opener. He states, "A mason can't be a good mason unless he knows the Holy Quran and follows its teaching."

With all this knowledge, I was still into my foul music. My group and I were hard partiers. One night we had a concert in Beaufort, SC. After the concert was over, me and my friends were riding around the dark streets of Beaufort high, and very much lost. We made lefts and rights for what seemed like forever before suddenly finding ourselves in a front yard with a sign that said JESUS SAVES. My high was blown. We quickly made a right turn and ended up on highway 170, which took us straight home. Nobody said a word in the car.

That little incident didn't stop me from getting high, but it did make me think. Instead of going to the club one weekend, I decided to kick back and enjoy my high in the studio while listening to a Led Zeppelin track entitled Stairway to Heaven. Then a weird thing happened as I was fooling around with an instrumental track that me and my cousin Maurice had laid down a couple months earlier. My hand began to write a song without me having any input. After I had written the lyrics I decided to record my vocals. I was tired, so I went home to crash without reviewing it. But the next day I went back to the studio to see what I had recorded: these were the words:

"As I sit in the cold and watch events unfold My Soul, Heaven... Eyes on fire, all my dreams and my desires, Heaven... Me and You what are we going to do? What are we going to do? As we sit and wait for Heaven... In the skies or in my mind Everyone has their own time, has their own time to get to Heaven .... This is my prayer, that one

15

day this Hell I am living in will become Heaven… And now I lay me down to sleep I pray to the Lord My soul to keep And if I die before I wake… Heaven"

This would be the beginning of me questioning whether getting high off smoking weed was the closest I was going to get to heaven. With all that I was learning, I still was living a foul lifestyle and these religions I'd been studying gave me no peace. Then one night all would change when a gun altercation caused me to wake up.

(Summer 2000) Oh, yes today is a good day. That was my thought as I headed to a party where you were expected to smoke to you choke. I was already in a good mood because on the way home from worker earlier, the Savannah radio deejay had been spinning one of our Cross Da Traxxx songs — Wanna Ride. When I pulled up in the yard for the party, police cars were everywhere. There was a gun altercation, and instead of relaxing smoking marijuana, this had suddenly turned into a night of pure drug drama. While sitting in the backyard with a 12-gauge shotgun on my lap, I had about an hour to really think about where I was, at this point in my life and how I ended up in this situation. I knew that night at the age of thirty-four that if I survived I would never be in this situation again.

Somehow, I had to change because, sadly, I had nothing to show for my years on the planet. That night ended with a brother dropping me off at my mom's house. He backed out of my driveway with his eyes totally closed. He was under the influence of weed and valium. As I watched a dead man back out of my yard my heart started pumping fast. I'm Done!

A couple days later I called my old boss in Virginia. (Walter Walker) Before I could say anything, he told me that God takes care of both babies and fools and that I was not a baby; he was basically telling me to straighten up. He gave me a job, and I started a couple days later. While in Virginia, I worked fifty to sixty hours a week and regularly chilled with my frat brothers, who were very supportive of my pursuit of producing hip hop music.

I also continued to study the occult still searching for truth. I went to a flea market in Newport News Va. and bought a CD by Obadiah 1. This CD expressed most of my thoughts and philosophies at the time. This brother was a follower of Dr. Malachi Z. York. Three months later I came home from the club hungover. While on my knees praying to a porcelain god I heard a message again this time I was instructed not to eat meat for thirty days. I followed that message, but didn't give up getting high. Half way into this fast, I found myself alone one day with a big bag of weed and some blunts. A young lady friend decided not to come over and get high with me. I smoked by myself and soon fell asleep. I woke up with a Bright Light in my living room blinding me. The Light left, and I was drug free. After a couple of days, it was as though my eyes just popped open and I could see what was going on all around.

This was the first time that I realized I was getting older. The streets and my party-like-a-rock star lifestyle were killing me slowly but surely. I went to work that morning. While walking through a building on campus I read a flyer about auditions for a theatrical play. I tried out and was cast alongside some very popular old school music and tv stars. When I read through the play, it felt as if I was reading my own life story. Nevertheless,

I shrugged off the personal effect the plot had on me and fell perfectly into my role because I knew how to act like a Christian. Rehearsal went from November through December, and during Christmas break I went back to South Carolina with three hundred 300 copies of my latest CD that I named PhilliyPhil Something. I was still into my music, but the only difference was that I was off marijuana.

On New Year's Eve 2001 I was at a local church having my car washed, and the young man, Lamonte Doe who washed my car invited me to church. I already knew that I was going to a party that night, but I lied to him and told him I might come. That night while heading toward the party, my cousin and I stopped for gas. I sold one of my PhilliyPhil Something records to a young female cashier, and when she paid I felt shame for selling this foul product to her. With the ten dollars in my hand, I asked her what she was doing tonight. "I'm going to church," she replied. "What?... Church?" Clearly, I was surprised. As we talked, I found out her church was the same church that I was invited to earlier. Well, that was enough for me to turn my truck around and head back in town to attend their midnight watch service. My cousin and his partner went on to the party. As soon as I stepped inside the church doors, I found it interesting that a few folks greeted me by my rap name, Philly Phil. I just returned the greetings and sat in the back. I was enjoying the service until I attempted to take off my jacket. That is when I realized that I had worn a shirt covered with fire-breathing dragons.

It was truly a wake-up call as I finally began to realize that I was working for satan with my foul music and my perverted lifestyle. I covered back up in shame and reluctantly sat through the rest of the service while the pastor preached about the importance of family. At the end of the sermon, he pulled all the families up front. Included was the Brother who washed my car and the young lady who bought my cd earlier. I was the only one still sitting and just watched as he prayed over the various families.

I could not wait to get out of there. When I got outside I took a deep breath and then decided right there on the spot to do a gospel album. It was the least I could do to put some balance in my life. As I traveled city to city with the Gospel Play Mommas Dees Girls I recorded gospel songs on my portable digital equipment back in my hotel room. I thought it was somewhat a good thing to be in a gospel atmosphere as I recorded my songs, but I was in for a bit of a surprise.

I already knew what Hollywood was like, but I did not expect this same kind of cut throat vibe as I toured with the other actors and actresses. The play Momma Dee's Girls started as a serious play, but by the time we were in Detroit, it was a drama/comedy. It didn't really feel like a gospel play at all. When I was let go/fired/cut in Detroit, honestly, it was relief.

At this point in my life, I was still living a double life. I wanted to do the right thing, but I was still very much filled with lust and clinging to all the crazy philosophies that I had learned over the years. While touring for the play, I had been doing my best to stay cool and on my best behavior. But after the first night in Detroit, I was approached by a middle-aged lady who took me to an after party. It really wasn't a party, but a dope house. I recognized where I was and quickly took my cash out of my wallet and put it into my sock. I made it back to the hotel but knew not to trip in these cities with these women that I did not know.

The next night I went to a club next to the hotel, and after a couple beers a young lady took me riding in her van. She was smoking a joint while driving, and after riding around, we came back to my room where we sat and talked for a while. I know my roommate thought I was crazy, so after I let her hear a couple of my gospel tracks, we bounced. I found out that she was having problems with her husband and trying to get out of her marriage. I attempted to comfort her but not with the love of God. I thank God that we did not have relations. Even though I was trying to follow Jesus, I had no power over my lust and desire for sexual gratification.

The lust that was in me drove me into the streets where I found a young lady who was willing to help me for some cash. This would be my last time making this type of transaction. I felt very bad afterword!

How does a man end up sleeping with a woman who sells her body? It does not happen overnight. The sexual appetite is awakened in a man through a lack of moral spiritual discipline, peer pressure from his friends, and through all the different forms of media. Fornication is a dangerous tool of the enemy. It can do serious damage to a person's body, mind and soul.

1 Corinthians 6 Know ye not that your bodies are the members of Christ? shall I then take the members of Christ, and make them the members of an harlot? God forbid. What? know ye not that he which is joined to an harlot is one body? for two, saith he, shall be one flesh. But he that is joined unto the Lord is one spirit. Flee fornication.

Save the Day (rhyme)

You are looking good, but that love is not for me. It is not worth losing family and my ministry. She got them goodies but them goodies is a straight trap. If you are feeling me, soldiers, let your soul clap. You don't really want to know what love is. You too busy on the block trying to feel what thug-life is. They are hollering, "Rap it Up!", thinking that it will not stop. Pop, it like it's hot, but it's ashes to ashes when those caskets drop. What about Herpes them rubbers can't stop THAT? Don't be confused; curiosity killed the cat. Don't even go there if you never been there. This game is dirty, and these players aren't playing fair. Promiscuous so many lovers that you don't know. And several of your partners living on the down low. How you doing your flesh done got turned-out. Ran up in Sodom and Gomorrah, took the wrong route. Thinking that you'll never ever make it back, not realizing that you're under a spiritual attack. Here it comes, the Word of God will save the Day. Yahshua is the Savior, waiting on you to pray......

Back in Hardeeville, I was in Wal-Mart to buy some music making material and ran into a young lady who asked me if I wanted to go to church. I brushed her off and kept stepping. I may have walked four steps when I heard something deep down inside of me convicting ME. I thought, "How are you going to make gospel music and you don't want to go to church?

I went to the church, and it was church like I had never seen before. People were crying, speaking in tongues, giving testimonies, and prophesying. I gave my testimony that night. And the pastor told me that I was a preacher. I doubted that, but she asked me to come back on Friday and do something for them. I thought she meant for me to sing, but when I got there the next Friday I realized that she wanted me to preach! I was shocked!

Now what was I going to say? I did not own a Bible. I only knew one verse and a couple of Christian songs. I asked God to help me and He did. I did not know what I was going to say but when I opened my mouth, words just flowed out. I did not have to think about what to say next. At the end of the presentation my mouth just closed, and I could not say another word and I sat down. They were so quiet that I thought I had done something wrong. But after about two minutes of complete silence, the pastor raised an offering and gave it to me. I stuffed all the envelopes into my music bag and went home. It was 2:30 in the morning when I woke my mother up and we counted the money then I said to my Mom this is what I was going to do for the rest of my life. It seemed like an easy way to make a living. Little did I know the price I was going to pay for that decision to preach the Gospel of Jesus Christ.

For the short amount of time I was at the church, I would just sit and listen. I remember one time the pastor was speaking about homosexuality, and in my mind, I was thinking how happy I was that I had never been involved in homosexuality at that very instant that I was thinking that, she said, "And masturbation is not of God either." I could have crawled under my chair. That was an alarm for me to examine myself. The stronghold of perversion was still a part of my life.

Many people, who are caught up in sexually perverted lifestyles, as I was, want you to point out in the Bible where it says that they should not do this and that: THOU SHALL NOT COMMIT MASTURBATION, thou shall not have anal and oral sex, Thou shall not sleep with your pets, grown men and women should never have sex with little boys and girls, etc. To those that believe that the Bible is true, let us go to the root and then we will deal with the fruit. And to those who don't believe the Bible is true, know that Yahshua loves you so much that He died on Golgotha to shed His precious blood for you and me.

2 Corinthians 10:4-5 (For the weapons of our warfare are not carnal, but mighty through God to the pulling down of strong holds;) Casting down imaginations, and every high thing that exalteth itself against the knowledge of God, and bringing into captivity every thought to the obedience of Christ;

I was only at this church for two weeks, but in that short period of time, I was shown love. I knew I was slowly changing. I then went to Atlanta to participate in the G.A.N.G. Conference 2001 at Bishop Eddie Long's church. I sold about twenty CDs on the first day in the lobby of New Birth and made enough to pay for a hotel room. I set up my music equipment in the church's cafeteria where all the vendors were set up and shared what God had done for me with anyone who would listen. Later, a young man from New York City who had returned a Source magazine he'd borrowed from me told me that his pastor wanted to talk with me. I was fine with that.

When I first saw the pastor, I saw an image of a gangster in pimp clothes with rings on every finger trapped in a stronghold of perversion, but when I looked again it was just a young man in a suit sitting down at a cafeteria lunch table. I thought I was having a weed flashback or something and it puzzled me. After our conversation he invited me to New York City to work with his choir. I agreed immediately.

One (rhyme)

We were One Long Before this world Began, who am I that you are mindful of Me, what is Man? a Living soul made of Flesh and bone. who knows that this world is not Our Home and one sweet day Sin and death will be Gone

Come The New Jerusalem Chief Cornerstone

Waking up with Just a simple touch of the Master's Hand... A consuming fire will Blaze across The Burning Sands, as we see the stars in Heaven shine in the Night, The Sun and The Moon were created By His Marvelous LIGHT

We were One Long Before this world Began, who am I that you are mindful of Me, what is Man? a Living soul made of Flesh and bone. who knows that this world is not Our Home and one sweet day Sin and death will be Gone

Come The New Jerusalem Chief Cornerstone

He created a Masterpiece with the Perfect timing of the Lord's Feast and the authority to resist and rebuke the Beast The sun will rise in the east but really it's just going around The Feast of Trumpets The Children of Yah will Hear That Sound Shofars in Zion tears of Joy Then No More Crying sickness lying or dying Yahshua Is Coming Back Brother P Just Prophesying and setting the record Straight, There's a wedding taking Place Yahveh Knows The Date Drinking The Fruit of the Vine with unleavened Bread will be on the Plate, Have Patience He's Worth The Wait ....)

After agreeing with the pastor from New York I walked outside of the New Birth cafeteria and could hear the speaker from the main building preaching about fraternity branding. I was very interested since I was branded all over my body with Omega brands. After his sermon I walked up to this minister, Bishop Terrell Murphy, and I could see the big horseshoe brand on his arm. How could I tell this man of God that I was in the same Fraternity? I was not ready to hear anything negative about the organization that held a very special dear and secretive place in my heart. I just gave him my CD and kept it moving.

Before we began our journey to New York City, we made a stop at Pastor Creflo Dollar's church to drop off some Jesus T-shirts. In the parking lot a brother asked me to pull out my sword. I told him I had no idea what he was talking about. He said, "Where is your Bible?" I told him I didn't have one. He shouted nicely, "How're you going to sing gospel music and don't have a Bible?" I just shrugged. But I knew that I was saved so I did not worry about what he had said. But it did make me think. I felt that something was off about this ministry in the beginning because they had six people in a seven-passenger van and no one jumped in my truck with me to help me drive. We left Atlanta around eleven 11 at night after being up all day for the last day of the G.A.N.G. youth conference 2001. I was in my truck, praying and listening to gospel music all the way.

We arrived in New York at 3:30 pm and hit traffic going to Long Island to the pastor's house. They dropped him off and did not ask me in, not even to use the bathroom. I just kept a smile on my face. 20 hours later finally we got to the church in Jamaica Queens at about eight pm. After a couple of hours, a group of guys showed up and my thought was that maybe they were having a late Friday night service. But then they told me they were going to the movies. The movies?

Our first stop was the Chinese food spot where the pastor paid for everybody's food to go. At the theater, we walked right past the ushers with no tickets, went inside and started tearing up that Chinese food. The movie, which was called Fast and Furious, started, but I was so sleepy I barely saw the first scene. At this point, it was about 2 am and I was put out with the co-pastor Elder Ron. After the movie, I returned to his house and instead of me having a bedroom, I was given some sheets and the living room couch. I couldn't really complain since the pastor had promised to take care of my room and board if I came.

Psalms 37:23 The steps of a good man are ordered by YHWH and he delighted in his way.

I just sucked it up like a soldier and figured that God had something for me in this city. New York was interesting. Young, single people made up most of the congregation. I could tell that the church leadership kept a tight grip on all the members. At first, I did not care because I was not a member. I was just there on assignment. I met the choir that I was to work with and I immediately knew the spirits that were controlling them. I told the co-pastor that they were full of pride and arrogance. He acknowledged my observation and told me that he wanted me to talk to them. I strongly felt it was the pastor's job to deal with his choir's attitude. After that incident the church helped me adjust to the city and basically left me alone. They gave me my first Bible, a small King James Version. I would read a little to go to sleep at night, starting with the red letters.

I met Sean Slaughter, the sound man for the church. His background was like mine. Sean was always on the road touring, doing gospel rap and working as a sound engineer. Sean came off the road to minister at the church summer concert/picnic. We were introduced, and after listening to some of my music he then invited me on stage with him to do a remix of one of his songs. At that same event I can remember asking the young people to raise their hands if they had ever been to a clinic for sexually transmitted diseases. I looked over the group and was astounded at the many raised hands. I thought while singing, America needs Yahshua more than ever.

While in New York, I had to get a job to meet my financial obligations. My first gig was at the Apollo in Harlem. I knew the keyboard player from the Gospel Play I was in, he got me a part time gig on the front door. Then I landed a full-time audio-visual tech job at the Marriott Hotel in Manhattan. I was on my way. I could not believe it.

The church was called Destiny Worship Center. Their pastor was Prophet Cohen and the co-pastor was Elder Ron, who knew the Bible back and forth. The praise team was awesome and services had some of the best singing that I had ever heard in church. The church also had these guys who were always around the pastor. During church services they would stand in the front the whole time, following the pastor's every move. My first impression was that they were security guards. But I soon learned that these men were armor bearers. I had no idea what armor bearers were.

I know the Bible tells us to put on the whole armor of God, but to me, this sounded like someone was holding your armor. How is this even possible? Was it part of the kingdom of Yahshua? Deep inside, I felt it was just people making stuff up.

Ephesians 6:11 says, "Put on the whole armor of God that ye may be able to stand against the wiles of the devil.

After the spies came back from exploring the land of Canaan, they were so intimidated by what they've seen that they came back with a report which discouraged any attempt or intent to go forth with the idea of conquering that land: they saw themselves as INADEQUATE ~ If we perceive things only through the natural eyes we might forfeit what's already ours but through faith, we'll say just like Joshua: We are well ABLE!

Many people have never dealt with drug dealers, players, hustlers, or pimps so when they come inside the church building, they probably don't have their guard up. But really, game is game no matter where it is played. There are probably hoodlums that have decided that the streets are too risky, so they have started churches as part of the trap to lure people in. Now, the church clubs are claiming that they are the covering for the people in their congregation. When in fact; they need to be covered by the blood of Yahshua. Friend, don't be deceived. Allow the Holy Spirit to open your eyes to the many tricks of the enemy.

That Spring 2001 I became celibate and decided that the next woman that I would become one with would be my wife. Up until this point I had been talking to a young lady I had met during the play Momma Dees Girl. She had just graduated, and we talked back and forth over the internet. I would tell her all the crazy stuff that was going on in the city. There was also another young lady, a recent graduate of Savannah State University, who I met in NYC at the public library. She lived around the corner from me and went to Greater Allen AME church. Since we both had bus and train passes, we often explored Manhattan together. Our most memorable trip was to the Statue of Liberty; we caught the E train to the World Trade Center and caught a boat to view the large statue. A month later, Sept 11, 2001.

The week before the bombing I had secured a job as an audio-visual technician at the Marriott in Manhattan. On Friday I called my supervisor and he informed me that they would not be able to let me start because the other Marriott hotel by the World Trade Center was destroyed. Well, my job went belly up. I had to scramble because my truck payment was three months behind.

By October I was working everyday as a New York City public school substitute teacher. I also was working part time as a programmer at the Queens public television studio. All the television stations were out that first week after the bombing. I found myself staring at the television set. I could hear some preachers talking but I could barely see their faces. I made out the local phone number at the bottom and called the church. The man asked me to come to the revival.

When I arrived, the people were praising the Lord and I joined in. The guest preacher was from Nigeria. Everybody at the church was real nice to me. I felt very comfortable even though I needed a translator most of the time. After the first night I decided that I wasn't going to stay at the church that brought me from Atlanta any longer. It was not working out and I made up my mind that if I had to I would sleep in my truck.

Sean told me if I needed a place to crash, then I could stay at his place until I got my own apartment. So that was it; I packed my stuff one night and just left. For me to break away was not that big of a thing because I was not a member of the church. In Jesus Christ I was still a baby and I knew it was time for me to mature. I went back to the church to talk with the Pastor. He tried to tell me why I should stay, but my season was up. And we parted ways.

This is Sister Karina's Testimony. She was one of the young ladies at the church when I came to New York. We worked together on a CD called the Tha Dungeon (2001)

The Introduction

Did I just join a cult? Hmmm. Many people will have you believe that you are weak and ignorant if you did. Joining a cult exposes us and makes us understand that many will come in his name to deceive. Not only to discern the wolves from the sheep, but also the goats from the sheep. (Luke warm vs. Believers of Christ). See, goats look like sheep, but you can tell them apart by what them consume. Goats eat anything in sight like trash, while sheep eat grass and clover (nature).

Know your so-called brethren by what he consumes, is it the word of Christ???

CONFUSION

As a child I grew up "Catholic", so my grandma calls it, I was exposed to Catholicism as well as Santeria and its traits. For those not familiar with Santeria, it is a mix of Roman Catholicism with African Voodoo. It was what the Africans slaves practiced when being forced to convert to Catholicism. They found a way to hide their african gods and conceal them with the Catholic saints (Example: Chango is Saint Barbara). At the age of 14 I read the bible yet "cleaned houses" using garlic, alcanfor, florida water, hopping over incense, carried holy water, wear my clothes inside out, did face readings and other forms of witchcraft to seek God. until I read a verse about witchcraft and mediums. I honestly believed because I wasn't doing palm readings and tarot cards, I was doing the will of God. I knew magic was wrong, but was lead to believe that "white" magic was good. I also got heavy into numerology. That is when I changed my name to Eleven. (High number in numerology)

SEEKING

Years past and I "got saved". My name Eleven now meant (1 one 1 relationship with Christ). I joined a Christian Club in College and they introduced me to a church called DWC. Here is where I met Brother P. I did not know him. He use to shout outside the church. "I smell big pimping". I thought he was crazy. Little did I know, he saw something in that church that he saw in his everyday life, a con artist hustling. That con artist was the Pastor. I also felt odd, but the sisters would have me believe that it was the devil tricking me. I had to stay. I had dreams of the pastor stripping off his clothes in church. I would have visions of him with women from the church. One fellow member said it was okay for him to watch nude film because he was our leader. Come to find out he was sleeping around and even got one pregnant. The church would fast, but he did not have to. No translation of tongues, I translated it but did not have the courage to speak "woe be unto you (church).

The truth

The Lord gave me many signs, yet I stayed. I daydreamed as the pastor lined everyone up according to how much their donation was. Large amounts got you hug or hi five from pastor. Brother P had left the church. I stayed and fasted until the Lord gave me a sign, and He did. The church lost its building and moved to a Calypso Club. I then began to feel alienated. I could not speak to anyone. Every night I dreamed and fasted. The last dream I had, the church had no roof, the pastor looked like a bum and the congregation was weak and thin. One day during sermon, the pastor spoke about me indirectly saying. Do you think your powerful? I knew my time was up. I had to go.

8 months later I bumped into a friend from the Christian Club, no longer a member of DWC, saying the church was gone. She said that on the last day of service the pastor went to the stage, put up his middle finger, laughed at everyone and said I am leaving to Florida, to a better church. I will be on TBN.

Leaders that repent are hard to find. What I have seen is that just like American businesses when one fails in running a successful business you just start another one. Sit down mighty man and woman of God and let the Lord restore you.

The revival at Eglise De Bethesada was still going on and I did not miss a night. After two or three weeks the Lord blessed me through the Pastor Rev Constance Pierre with a basement apartment. I went to work early in the morning and stayed at the church until they closed the doors. I only came home to sleep and wash.

One evening the preacher from Nigeria came back to that church and was praying for people in the congregation. As he passed me he barely laid his hand on my cheek and boom. I went flying backwards. I jumped up, not having any idea what had happened.

After the service was over, his wife prayed for me and all I remember was being thrown in the air and landing on my head. I knew that my head was bleeding. As I tried to get up a force just knocked me out on the floor. Lying face down, When I finally got up, I just walked outside. I can remember my exact thoughts, which were to go back to my basement apartment and find out who Jesus is according to the scriptures. I went back and grabbed my little black Bible and began to devour it. It was as though I had never read this stuff. I could understand the words now, plus I did not get sleepy. Now instead of reading the Bible like a sleeping pill, I love reading this living book. My mind was being renewed by the power of the scriptures.

I AM (Teaching)

I was now devouring the scriptures. My first lesson in that basement apartment would come from the gospel of John. In chapter 8 Jesus was confronted by the religious men of the day. He had told them that if Abraham was your father then you would love Me. And he went on to tell them that their father was satan.

Jesus finally said that Abraham rejoiced to see him. They were like you are not even 50 years old and Abraham died a long time ago. And that when Jesus dropped the bomb on them. He said Before Abraham I AM. No more words were said They picked up stones to kill him for what they felt was blasphemy.

That's when I had to dig back into the Torah to find who Abraham was dealing with that might be like the Messiah. And that when I came across Melchizedek in Genesis. This Priest of the Most High was defined by the book of Hebrews as The King of Righteousness and The King of Peace! In My mind I was like that is the Old Testament appearance of Yahshua /Jesus. Yahshua was bigger than the baby in the manger. He was not only The Passover Lamb, but he also was The Word that was with God and The Word that was God. Immanuel God with Us. Now I understood the Royal Priesthood of the believer. We the Body of the Messiah Yahshua are together a Kingdom of Priest. We are The Light of the World with Yahshua as our High Priest, The Head of the Body. The Levitical Priesthood had changed and so has the Law changed.

For this is the covenant that I will make with the house of Israel after those days, saith the Lord; I will put my laws into their mind, and write them in their hearts: and I will be to them a God, and they shall be to me a people:

And they shall not teach every man his neighbour, and every man his brother, saying, Know the Lord: for all shall know me, from the least to the greatest. For I will be merciful to their unrighteousness, and their sins and their iniquities will I remember no more.Hebrews 8

Every day I was growing stronger in the written word. And I could not wait to fellowship with brothers and sisters in and out of church. One day after work I went by the church and a Seventh Day Adventist preacher was doing a video. I just sat and watched, not really understanding what it was all about. And then I saw him doing sign languages that the fraternities use.

I made the decision to talk to him when he finished about those gestures. Later, we talked by the side of the building and he told me that he was former freemason. He said the the God of the Bible was not the god of the Lodge. I said, "Well, what does that have to do with me? I'm a Que. He said that he knew of the black Greek lettered organizations and that our rituals and initiations came from the organization that he used to be a part of, the freemasons. I went home distraught. But two weeks later after heavy contemplation, I went to my Chevy truck and unscrewed the Omega license plate off the front. Strangely, I felt a weight lift off my shoulders. The Soul Tie was Cut. I really did not think to much of it. I knew of a couple of brothers who were no longer active in the fraternity because of their faith. I knew these brothers but never talked to them about leaving the frat.

Oh Watchman (Prophecy)

Oh Watchman, Oh Watchman, Watchman on the wall-
Secure the gates, sound the alarm. Gird up your loins with
My Truth and blow the Trumpet. Tell My people, tell them
I AM coming. Guard the gates and watch upon the wall for
the enemy, for he sneaks in at the gateways and tries to
slide through the windows. Bar the gates; secure the
windows, cry out in the streets & warn My people "I" Am
coming - I Am coming" - don't let the enemy rob, steal,
kill, & destroy the hope, the joy, the life, the deliverance I
have for my children. I give life abundant; hope & joy -
Tell My people - I Am coming. I have placed arrows in
your quiver & keys in your hand. Use them as I instruct,

Find the mark, send the arrow - strike with the sword;
Speak my Word & drive the enemy out the door. Then turn
& speak life to that dead situation. Oh Watchman,
Watchman, guards my gates - sound the Trumpet- keeps
my city until I come.

Secret Society Mentality

To understand the underground black Greek fraternity
mentality let's go back to the summer before my senior
year in college, I went to the P/R Military Society picnic at
F.A.M.U. This is where I received my first brands. I tried
to pledge Omega every year since 1986 but it just wasn't
my time, so I made the decision to go for it again after I
graduated.

After graduation I decided to drive my mom to
California to live with her sister. Once I got out there I
found a job working for the City of Riverside. I met some
grad Omega brothers out there and went on line with a guy
in the army. We visited the brothers for a month or so and
finally were approved to go on line.

On the first night of line they snatched us and took us in a room where they explained that there was a change in the fraternity called Membership Intake. I told my line brother that I could not become a paper member on the west coast. I got to go home and get down the right way.

While all this was going on, I had started making more Christian music. My rap name was MC REV, and I was doing positive Christian raps in the clubs and at school assemblies. I really enjoyed it and decided to go back to Hampton for a Master's Degree while pursuing a Christian music career. Before that could happen, a brother who worked in the media production department at Hampton University gave me a job as an audio-visual tech. After shooting my first music video. I loved it and decided to switch careers.

While working at Hampton University, I hooked up with my old buddies that had already crossed, and they put me on line with three other guys. After pledging hard for about two weeks, shedding blood, sweat and tears, they dropped all of us because of some crazy stuff. I decided never again to pledge illegally underground unless I was legit with the documentation(Paper).

Paper is a term that is used to explain a member of the black Greek lettered organizations who did not go through an **underground** process. After being a member of the fraternity for about a week and a half, we were officially on-line underground. After five weeks, one of my line brothers and I could not believe that we were still on line. I almost quit because it didn't seem fair, but we knew that if we did not see it through, then our names would be mud. We stuck it out and a week later we crossed the burning sands. After a year in the fraternity I remember one summer sitting down and writing several short stories and poems. One poem I wrote was called Purple and Gold Hell. The last line said, as surely as there is a purple and gold heaven, there is a purple and gold hell.

Black Greek lettered Organizations are barely 100 years old and members are so dedicated to the societies that they will not only break the law by hazing new members. But as I did they will take branding irons usually hangers and burn the greek letters into their flesh. The smell of burning flesh is unforgettable and on this side, I would now definitely say that it is an ungodly practice. Many people outside refer to the underground aspect of BGLO's as educated gangs. Move wrong around some of these chapters and you can seriously get hurt. The way that we treated the ladies is very shameful. These underground practices along with the cursed oaths and ungodly soul ties with unbelievers are some of the reasons why the fraternities and sororities in the BGLO's are so angry prideful violent.

28 Ye shall not make any cuttings in your flesh for the dead, nor print any marks upon you: I am the LORD.

29 Do not prostitute thy daughter, to cause her to be a whore; lest the land fall to whoredom, and the land become full of wickedness. Leviticus 19

I have met several members who have not gone through the barbaric hazing and most of them I have met are no different than meeting members of the NAACP or Urban League. In Hindsight Membership Intake was a good idea but 25 years later and the official process has in no way eliminated the Underground Alter Ego Shadow Orgs.

One of the plays that I had written was called **The Underground** and was loosely based on my underground reality in the fraternity. I was the Dean of Pledges, and as the Dean of Pledges you are responsible for the guys coming into the fraternity what we considered the right way. One night, the frat house was full of brothers, and the pledges were going through a water ritual, which is when we make the pledges drink gallons of water. While one of my pledges was drinking water, a big brother punched him right in the middle of the chest. The blow was not that bad but the timing of it sent the pledge straight into an epileptic seizure. Suddenly, the brothers were ghost. That is the day when I knew there was no real love in the underground. Three of us stayed with the young man. But we were so crazy that we did not even take him to the hospital.

Out of all the conversations that I had trying to get in the fraternity and while I was in the fraternity. I could count on my hand when that conversation had anything to do with faith in Jesus Christ. I remember at Hampton University sitting in the chapel on Sunday Morning with pledgees sitting in the sanctuary on Line. I always thought that was strange. This could only be done in churches that do not believe in the operation of the gifts of the spirit. But today even the Holy Ghost churches are having to deal with people wanting to be in secret societies and at the same time serve in the church.

In the Original COGIC church the leadership openly spoke out against the freemasons.

"Mother taught the Word of God in power, against Lodges, exposing their rituals. She was imprisoned, rotten-egged, and beaten for this"

http://www.cogic.org/womensdepartment/about-us/our-history/

In the Assembly of God fellowships they have information in their bylaws against joining secret societies.

"Article IX of the Assemblies of God Bylaws includes an entire section on advising against membership in secret orders."
https://ag.org/Beliefs/Topics-Index/Secret-Societies

The Play that you will read here is the same as it was in my book that I had written almost 2 decades ago except that the strong language has been edited as to reflect my Faith as a follower of Yahshua

Prayer

This prayer is for the weak caught up in the struggle

This prayer is for the hustler who really don't want to hustle

This prayer is for the righteous muscle coming down from that spiritual throne were 24 elders are casting crowns ...

This prayer is for the new saints don't faint receive the Holy Ghost and go hard in the paint ...

This prayer came from my savior and it's yours if you're his ,get covered by the blood and let him handle your biz

This prayer is about forgiveness no need to hold a grudge the name is brother p commissioned from foundation to show love ...

This prayer is for knowledge wisdom and understanding This prayer is for the bruhs still hazing and branding

This prayer is for the Hindus Muslims Jews and Christians when the Creator calls your name you better listen....

This prayer for all those who were sexually abused who may not even know that they are sexually confused ...

This prayer is for the elders to protect the sheep seed time and harvest we sow we reap ...

This prayer is from Yah to those who don't know how to pray never give up Yahshua is the Way.

THE UNDERGROUND

"those who know will not tell, those who tell do not know"

THE UNDERGROUND is a story about black Greek lettered fraternities. This story is fiction - all characters and situations were made up in my head. This story was inspired, however - by the death of a young man in 1992, and is based upon an underground attitude that I was introduced to as a freshman in 1984.

Setting: Newark, New Jersey

Upsilon Lions - A Black secret society for men with college degrees

BROTHERS of Upsilon

Dr. Perry Ellis President of the Upsilon Lions

Jerome Haynes Underground Dean of Pledges (DP)

Big Percy The Dean of Discipline

SuperCat Mac Daddy Minister of Information

Big Brother Break 'Em Off Sum 19-year-old neophyte from Winston-Salem State University

MAIN PLEDGEES

Jack Hampton University Graduate Native of Newark, New Jersey/Age 21

Brian North Carolina A&T Graduate Native of New York, New York Age 22

Michael Norfolk State University Graduate Native or Hampton, working in New York/Age 22

Bill Virginia State University Graduate Native of Detroit, working in New Jersey/Age 23

40

Gerald University of California/Los Angeles Graduate Native of Newark, New Jersey/Age 21

Mr. James Watson Tuskegee University Graduate Newark, New Jersey Business Man/Age 47

Mr. Mario Stevens Savannah State Graduate Newark, New Jersey Retired Military Man/Age 50

The first scene takes place at the Panhellenic Step Show. The Upsilon Lions step and do an incredible job for an older Graduate Chapter. The crowd loves them.

Percy: Man, I'm getting too old for this ....

Jerome: Yeah, but we still can "move the crowd", baby . . .

Super Cat: All the ladies were screaming for me!!

Jerome: Hey, Brothers - I'm out of here. I'll see y'all at my apartment tomorrow. Peace!

The second scene takes place at Jerome's apartment. He is sitting by himself reminiscing. One event sticks out in his mind more than any other. It is of a time when he was a new member of Upsilon Fraternity. He went to the FREAKNIC Spring Celebration in Atlanta, not knowing how crazy the Brothers of Upsilon were . . . While walking around enjoying all the beautiful women, Jerome notices a group of Upsilon Brothers:

Jerome: What's up Frat?

Upsilon Brother 1: What's up, where you from?

Upsilon Brother 2: Yeah, where you from, Bruh?

Jerome: I'm from the Newark, New Jersey Graduate Chapter.

Upsilon Brother 3: GRADUATE CHAPTER! Oh, I know you didn't pledge! Did you pledge? Did you pledge?

Jerome: Of course, I pledged!!

Upsilon Brother 4: If you pledged, then why did the chicken cross the street?

Jerome: Get out of here with that Betty Crocker Made up challenge; I don't have to tell you anything!

Upsilon Brother 1: You going to tell us something, or that shirt is coming off your back!

Jerome: If anyone touches me, I . . . huh?

Before Jerome could say another word, he was jumped by the four Brothers. When he awakened, he was shirtless. The Brothers had knocked him out and left him for dead. From that day on, he knew to always be on alert around Brothers.

His daydreaming is broken up by the doorbell. Percy and Super Cat arrive ready to get to the business of taking care of business. The Business of Pledging:

Jerome: What's up Frat? How the brethren doing?

Percy: What's up Cat Daddy? The brothers are ready to rock 'n roll, so lock and load.

Super Cat: Yes, I can't wait, Man. I haven't swung wood in a long time.

Percy: Yeah, I'm a little rusty, but since Jerome is the Dean, I might not be able to put in work for Upsilon.

Jerome: Hey, these guys are not just going to walk into the Frat!

Percy: Yeah, that's Bullcrap!

Super Cat: If we let them skate and skip the hazing, they'll take the Frat for granted. They won't love Upsilon!

Percy: I don't know why they got rid of pledging'. It ain't anything wrong with making a person work for something.

Jerome: Think about it - you know why they got rid of pledging . . . because Brothers have no self-restraint or self- control. They lose their mind around pledgees. That's why we must be extra careful this year.

Percy: Don't get soft on me, Jerome.

Jerome: I'm not, just more responsible. Sometimes I wonder if we are no better than street gangs in Chicago or California, damn!

Super Cat: How in the world can you compare Upsilon with a gang, Negro? You are tripping!

Jerome: Who you calling a Negro?

Super Cat: You, Negro. You have a problem with that?

Percy: Huh?

Super Cat: Don't worry about that, he's just tripping to avoid the gang issue.

Jerome: Hold up. I'm not avoiding anything. Gangs are territorial, frats are territorial. Some gangs brutally haze their new members. Some frats brutally haze their new initiates. Some gang members travel in packs for protection. Some frat brothers travel in packs for protection. So Super Cat, you tell me the difference.

Super Cat: We do community service. Gangs sell dope to the community. We stress educational achievement. Gangs stress making money 'by any means necessary'. We have respect for our elders. Gangs have only respect for power. Must I go on?

Jerome: No, no you've made your point. All I'm saying is, we don't have to dehumanize a man by abusing our power as big brothers. This process should be used to make these young men into leaders who will give back instead of just taking.

Percy: That's all good, but how are we going to bring these young men into the fold?

Super Cat: The right way!

Jerome: What do you mean, the right way?!

Super Cat: I mean we must break them down and build them up in the ways of Upsilon.

Percy: Yeah Baby, that's what I'm talking' about.

Super Cat: See, this is tradition. This is how it is supposed to be.

Jerome: Our Founders would turn over in their graves if they knew of this activity. Don't get me wrong. I'm down with the underground, but remember-brutal hazing was not a part of our humble beginnings.

Super Cat: So, Jerome, what's up? How we going to do this?

Jerome: We will use PT, physical training, to reinforce the information and the only contact will be with wood in the cut. No smacking, slapping, punches or spitting on. If you are caught, there will be strict discipline enforced.

Scene 3 takes place at the First National Bank at 10:00pm on Saturday. It is the Official Crossing Ceremony for the inductees under the new No Pledge Program.

Dr. Ellison: As the President of the Upsilon Lions, I am glad to see men still striving for honor and truth - our motto. As of this day you seven men are officially Lions of Upsilon! Congratulations!

Later that night five of the new members get together to discuss their immediate futures as members of Upsilon:

Jack: Man, this is Bull! We didn't do nothing to get in! We skated! I don't feel like an Upsilon Lion! I feel like a sucker who just got jacked for one thousand dollars.

Michael: No No! No!!

Brian: The brothers were treating us like we really didn't deserve to be brothers.

Michael: We really don't deserve it. My Dad pledged for three months. My brother even pledged for six weeks, 2 years ago. We didn't do anything! But pay 1,000 dollars!

Bill: Calm down. Listen, I know some of the younger brothers who are willing to take us through the old school way, so that we can survive without worrying about brothers attacking us everywhere we go!

Jack: Forget that, Bill. If a dude touches me, brother or not, he will get smoked, shot straight up you understand.

Bill: By attacking Jack, I mean harassing you whenever you sport your gear or attend functions sponsored by the bro's.

Gerald: I've sat back and listened to all your complaints. I'm not letting no one whip me. Pledging is illegal. They voted this new process in and if brothers can't deal with it, they can kiss my attaché case. I have a job and a business to take care of. No time for playing ego games.

Bill: Cool, Gerald. I understand how you feel. It's not your fault that the process is weak. I can dig it, but check this- I'm still going to go underground and who's ever with me- meet me at my apartment in East Orange tomorrow night. Peace, Brothers. *The next night, everyone showed up - except Gerald.*

Brian: I knew that punk wasn't with it. I didn't trust him from the giddy-up.

Jack: Why?

Brian: Because he went to that white school on the west coast.

Michael: Yeah, he's not used to this Black Panther like business.

Jack: I think the Panthers started on the West Coast in fact Huey P the founder was a member of the elite eight and earned all his degrees from Predominantly White Institutions of Higher Learning.

Bill: You see, we all come from black colleges and if you didn't go hard, you didn't get any respect on the yard. That's how it is up and down the east coast. Easy don't get any respect. *Bill calls Jerome on the phone*

Hello, Jerome, It's Bill. Me and three of my boys are trying to do a little something. What's up?

Jerome: Don't say anything else. Get over my house right now. *They all get in the same car and drive to Jerome's house. Jerome: Jack, Brian, Michael and Bill* - I want you to know is that it won't be easy. We are not going to let you get hurt but we will give a program that will make you proud to be an Upsilon Lion.

In two nights you are to meet me back here in pledge gear which includes army boots, blue jeans, t-shirts, sweatshirts, matching drawers and socks, and an army field jacket. Alright, remember loose lips sink ships. Get out of here. *Two nights later, they are back knocking at the door.*

Jerome: Get in here shoulder to shoulder. Don't say a word. From now on you will be referred to as kittens and you will answer all Big Brothers of Upsilon Chapters as

Sir. Yes, Sir and no Sir. Just like the army. This is Boot camp. Now, drop and give me 40, kittens!

Jack: Jerome, I mean excuse me Sir, can I take a leak?
Jerome: No, pee in your pants!

Super Cat: I am Super Cat, the Mac Daddy Lion. In charge of information. Here is your pack. You have a week to learn every poem, song, and piece of history.

Brian: Excuse me, Sir Cat Daddy.

Super Cat: Shut up, Kitten. My name is Super Cat the Mac Daddy. If you mess up, my name or my information, I will personally create a bad day for you kittens. Understand me?

Pledgees: Yes Sir.

Percy: My name is Big Percy, known to keep a kitten on the edge. Ready to jump off the ledge. This here with the help of my brothers is an underwater aqua boogie affair, and if you cannot swim, you're bound to drizzown. I oversee discipline. Get out of line and your behind is mine. Do you Kittens understand?

Pledgees: Yes Sir.

Jerome: Now, y'all are about to go-but before you raise up out of here we must introduce you to the Kitty Kat Breaking, Lion taming, rod of discipline, cut from the root of a redwood tree in Ethiopia. Are you ready for this?

Pledgees: Yes Sir.

Jerome: Big brother Percy, would you please do the honors?

Percy: It would be my pleasure, and remember-Kittens, this is going to hurt me worse than it is going to hurt you.

Jerome: Do you believe that?

Pledgees: No Sir!

Jerome: What?!

Pledgees: Yes Sir!

In the car on the way to Michael's apartment where the line brothers stayed.

Jack: Man, them dudes are crazy! Big Percy tried to kill us with his illiterate self!

Bill: You must stay focused. Don't think about the pain!

Brian: That's bull! My rear end is throbbing I can't even think straight!

Bill: They may call you a Kitten, but you don't have to be one, Brian.

Brian: Forget you!

Michael: Everybody chill out. You must admit Bill, that mess is crazy!

Bill: Yeah - it's crazy, but don't let it get to you. This is nothing compared to what people used to get. Think of it that way.

Brian: What they went through was bull, too. I can't do this anymore!

Jack: From now on, you will be known as an eternal kitten. You don't want that, do you?

Brian: Well, no, but if I got to get beat down to be a brother - then forget being their brother and if I lose a friend because I didn't go underground - he wasn't a friend in the first place.

Jack: Well, you will always be my line brother, but I'm still staying underground.

Michael: Me too, B.

Brian: You too, Bill?

Bill: You know it! Brian: Well, take me home because I'm Audi 5000. Tell Jerome, Big Percy, Cat Daddy to kick rocks. Peace!

This statement was said as they drop Brian off.

Bill: I guess it's just us now. 3 the hard way.

Jack and Michael sigh as they drive home for a couple of hours of sleep before work. Three weeks later, 3 the hard way was almost finished. They had two more days to go.

Unbeknownst to them, they had reached the point where they were a team working together to accomplish all tasks. Pain was mental. The next night would be a night they would not forget. It was midnight at the local high school football field. The Line was made to run around the track until there were exhausted,

and then they were blindfolded and left standing in the field for two hours. Then there was P.T. for an hour. After all this, they were thrown in the car belonging to Big Percy and taken back to Jerome's house where they met Big Brother Break 'em off some.

Jerome: I would like to introduce to you kittens to a brother from way down south where the green grass grows.

BBB: How you kittens doing?

Pledgees: Fine Sir   *BBB goes to slap Jack and Bill instantly take the blow.*

BBB: I like that. Looking out for your line brother. *(Then he sucker punches Bill)* BBB: Ah, too quick for you kittens. Well, that's okay. For the next hour, big brother *(punches Michael)* - that's right - big brother huh? *For the next hour BBB grills the line mentally and physically.*

49

BBB: You guys are alright. There's one last thing and I'm gone. He brings out 5 gallons of water and he tells then to finish it in 10 minutes or he will be whipping kittens all night.

They pass the water up and down the line. After 4 gallons Jack starts to shake and passes out.

BBB: Another one bites the dust.

Jerome: Chill out, BBB. Something is wrong.

BBB: Oh, he just passed out. He will be up and about tomorrow. You Negros are alright with me. Bill, Michael - here is my number. Call me when you cross the burning sands. See ya'll. I'm out!

Bill notices that Jack's pulse is low and alerts Jerome and Big Percy.

Bill: Something is wrong. We better take him to a hospital.

Big Percy: You cannot do that!

Jerome: Forget that, Percy. Something is wrong!

Super Cat: Take him out of those boots and line gear, and put on some regular clothes - then take him.

It takes a long time to switch the clothes because Jack was a large brother and limp. His clothes were everywhere by the time they got him to the hospital. Michael was freaking out"!

Michael: He dead, man! He is dead, man!

Bill: Shut up and park, so we can get in the Emergency Room.

Jack was pronounced DOA dead on arrival. An Emergency meeting was called the next day. The brothers wanted to know what happened. Jerome made the announcement that Jack went to step practice, then passed out later that night. The same reason was given to the hospital and his parents. An autopsy was done, and bruises were found all over Jack's light skinned body; his rear end was black and blue with callouses.

Brian: Yo! What up fellas? What in the world is going on? Jack was my Man!

Bill: I know, Brian.

Brian: Well, what happened?

Michael: Calm down.

Brian: Calm down, what happened?

Bill: You know, after step practice, he came back here and passed out.

Brian: Bull, Bill, because you know, and I know that he was healthy as an OX

Michael and Bill sigh.

Brian: Those suckers made you guys drink lots of water then whipped your butts and he could not take it. That is what happened!

Bill: No, no - you got it all wrong.

Brian: Well, listen to this. Jack's Mom is suing the fraternity and heads are going to roll on this one. You better remember our fraternity's motto; —Honor and Truth and by that autopsy report, a lot of stuff was going on that night: contrary to the truth that you are saying. (Brian leaves).

Michael: Yo Bill, Brian was right man. We got to tell the truth to protect the honor of our fraternity.

Bill: Are you out of your mind? If we tell what really happened that night the fraternity will get sued, and we will be kicked out of what we worked this hard to get into. The truth is what we make it.

Michael: So, when officials lie to stop riots or when Oliver North sold weapons behind the country's back to help brothers kill brothers in Nicaragua, it's alright - cause the falsehood is for a higher cause.

Bill: Yes, that's what I'm saying. Look at all the people who stood up for the truth: Martin Luther King - the wrongness of Vietnam - Dead. Malcolm X - after the trip to Mecca - dead. Even Jesus Christ with his divine truth, dead, dead, dead. All murdered for revealing the truth. You've got to play the game or get played. It's as simple as that.

Michael: Yeah, we must play the game, but this game has turned deadly, and Jack wasn't revealing a thing.

Bill: Whatever we do, Michael - me and you have got to stick together.

The next scene takes place at church during the funeral. As the ceremony begins, the soloist sings, "Don't Cry For Me".

The family can't help themselves. Bill, Michael, Brian, and Gerald try to comfort the mother outside of the church as she loses her composure. Brian hugs her, she pulls away yelling:

Mother: No! No! Why did you and your fraternity have to kill my son? Why? He never hurt anybody! Why? Why?

Father: Let her be, son. My wife is hurting deep inside. Jack was our only child.

After the funeral, the brothers of Upsilon went over to Brother Percy's house for dinner.

Michael: Percy, I want you to know - why you let that visiting brother make us drink all that water.

Percy: Listen, you didn't have to drink it.

Michael: Yeah, right. You know that's bull!

Bill: Percy, if we would have said no to the water, we would probably still be getting paddled by Big Brother Break 'Em Off Some.

Super Cat: Ya'll should have manned up!

Bill: Drop dead, Super Cat. Our line brother is dead because we put our lives in your hands.

Jerome: Bill, you are absolutely right. I messed up as Dean, and Jack died - but we didn't plan for him to die. I should have never allowed the brothers to give him that much water online. Damn!!

As Jerome realizes his guilt, FBI Agents break into the home. Michael jumps up and states that he is an agent and that Bill, Super Cat, Percy and Jerome are under arrest for participation in illegal activities.

Big Brother Break 'Em Off Sum is arrested in North Carolina - and Brian was picked up at his mother's house in New York as an accomplice. Percy punches Michael and is quickly subdued by the agents. Bill was in shock! He couldn't believe that Michael had betrayed him and the fraternity. Michael was an FBI Agent who was working with the National Upsilon Lions to crack the underground process that was performed nationwide. Criminal charges were brought against the seven young men. Michael released all his journals to the Federal Prosecutor so that he could set his case up against the young men. Two months later, the court case rolls around. The charges are as follows: Bill - Illegal hazing activity Brian - Illegal hazing activity Super Cat - Illegal hazing Percy - Illegal hazing Jerome - Second degree murder Big Brother Break 'Em Off Sum - Second degree murder

Bailiff: All rise for the Honorable Judge Douglas Perot.
Judge: Could you fine gentlemen please make your arguments?

Defense: Your Honor and distinguished members of the jury, the prosecution has a journal to present to you, but that's not what this trial is all about. Tradition and rites of passage is what this is about. My client may have unknowingly broken a few rules but did not; in anyway think that Jack Johnson's life was in jeopardy. These men are productive, intelligent, law abiding and tax paying citizens who may have made some mistakes in judgment but by no means do they belong in jail with drug dealers, murderers, thieves and junkies.

Prosecution: Your Honor, men and women of the jury, this case is not about tradition. This is a case about men knowingly breaking the law - pure and simple. When they broke the law, it had fatal consequences. The same fatal consequences that the law was trying to avoid.

Judge: Will the prosecution please call their first witness?

Prosecution: The State calls Michael Smith to the stand.

Bailiff: Do you solemnly swear to tell . . .

Prosecution: Could you explain what happened when you went undercover to join the Upsilon Lions fraternity?

Michael: Like I said in my journal - Jack died of exhaustion, stress, and too much water from Big Brother Break 'Em Off Sum during an illegal pledge session.
Prosecution: The state rests.

Judge: Your witness, defense.

Defense: All that sounds good, but I have these men who say that what you have said is a lie. Why should the jury believe you over them?

Michael: After the funeral - Bill, Super Cat, Percy, Jerome and I ate dinner together.

Defense: So - What does that have to do with this case?

Michael: I was wired, and I have the tape right here if the Bailiff would be so kind as to play it . . . *They play the tape.*

Defense: You Honor, may I approach the bench? We would like to change our plea. **THE END**

After the Israelites *wandered in the wilderness for forty years, they were finally close to enter the Promised Land but there was one more barrier in their way: THE JORDAN RIVER... AND once again, God shown up with all might and power, they crossed over on dry land... ~ He*

is the same yesterday, today & forever; at this stage of the game you need to TRUST him more than ever before and just STEP OUT on FAITH!

Pharaoh Let My People Go saints aint going to take it no more Sound off the shofars for victory The deaf will hear and the blind will see They will see the Day of the Lord they will See...Out of Egypt walked over on Dry land following Moses Just Like we Follow the Son of Man and into the desert the wilderness of sin 40 years or 40 days there's only one way to win to eat the bread of life and drink the living water that flows from the rock of all ages only Yah knows How this story goes and Oh it is written all in his word the Passover lamb of Yah that take away the sins of the world Rose on the third in the name of Yahshua

Christian individual (rhyme)

You were a Christian individual then you did the ritual cross the burning sands and hazing became habitual…Why you walking with a brick in your hand? 32 degrees freeze you are a baby man. goats ride camels while you stand still at the base. Your blindfold is invisible a Pyramid is in your face. the top is on your ones now you have a third eye. the only way to survive homie is your flesh has got to die. Awake o Sleeper and arise from the DEAD The mind of Yahshua is trying to get up in your head. The Comforter is here to lead you into the Truth… Go Back to how you was raised Go back to the God of your youth …And if you never knew the Creator of the Universe the Blood of Yahshua was shed to take away the curse …I dig your afrikan/kemetian mumbo jumbo ritualistic gumbo I must stay humble never rumble as your tower of Babel crumbles Pink Floyd said it best when he sung another brick in the wall… baby chickens learning to crawl when I stumbled upon the final call…let's take it back to 85 where loose lips would always sink ships nose wide open smelling hips stealing for the brothers while burning my fingertips …religion is all I had and I lost that like Tupac Shakur …aids has no cure? but the faith I have is pure I smell a bucket of manure a foul stench it's the Grinch all spirits are not the same game recognize game The Blood of Yahshua can heal the broken hearted and Lame In order to see the kingdom of Yah you must be born Again I am not your enemy and one day you may greet me as a friend. Wake up brother you are dreaming with visions of blaspheming a nightmare is screaming the product of clay is called seamen I see men who want to be god but they will and must die these dudes don't care about you they'll leave you where you lie but the God that came in the flesh was walking in the Garden hearts begin to harden as

Governors sign your pardon from state to state useless the 20 bars are not physical I'll spit out 20 more just to show you it gets critical analytical my thesis is not written on paper an inward circumcision got spectators catching the vapors some serious haters wrestling with pinc alligators get out the way and let the players play in the Himalayas all day

I keep it 100 at 51 I worship the Son of the living God while you worship the sun check Romans 1

that's how it got perverted and twisted …twist it back before it's too late and you hollering I missed it.

Born Again in a Black Greek lettered Organization by the spirit we must be Lead. don't trip off what he said, or she said rebuke the rumors in your head your seeing red but chill relax take a little water I am not here to harm I look at you like sons and daughters

You sinners got plenty networks why monkey up in here? Rebellion is as witchcraft the donkeys up in here. Numbers 22 especially for you insider goat riders for those who spark lighters, rhyme biters and dog fighters

Why come showing your emotional side? The words will never hide what's going on inside. Living for Yahshua is an ice-cold decision without permission double minded brains cause division

Sorry dude you can't have it both ways. worship and praise I blaze trails for those in a daze and bay bay bayz

But Brother P the pharaoh stuff is so cool, the ankhs, and the Egyptian tombs, the bananas, gorillas, the nasty hip

hop tunes we like strolling and you know we do plenty community service chill homie Relax,

Yahshua Saves maybe that's why you so Minervous.

Brother P's TestimonyTract

This is my living testimony and I say to others—you are not alone. Many have come out of Black Greek Lettered organizations because of their personal relationship with Jesus Christ. We will continue to pray for our brothers and sisters inside and outside of these organizations.

I was a nasty Q – dog/ Omega man ... let me give a real testimony out of love for all of God's children in and out of secret societies. After six years of failed attempts to cross the burning sands into Omega land, I finally crossed in spring of '92. My pledge process that took place in the years '86- '91 contained more hazing than intake processes nowadays.

Broken teeth and arms, and near-death experiences were all part of being a Q in the era I lived in. This was the time that a young man from Norfolk State dropped line and sued the fraternity. Back then to me he was wrong. I viewed him as a betrayer—a sell-out. But this young man was a gospel singer whose jaw was broken by one of his big brothers, an Omega who was taking part in initiating those on line. I was also beat down and did plenty of beating. During my time as an Omega, I served as an ADP and DP (Assistant Dean of Pledges and Dean of Pledges). I have abused and mistreated women

I also have witnessed women being sexually abused. When I was a nasty Q-dog, my attitude was —they wanted it. Today, I carry scars, a broken wisdom tooth, and brands on my chest, arms, and legs. I gave up blood, sweat, and tears for Omega... I remember before I crossed two brothers quit the frat because of religious convictions, but the other brothers kept it on the down low.

Those two brothers never came back to witness to us. Those of us in the fraternity just put it out of our minds. That following summer my best friend, an Alpha man, was getting married and his wife, who is a member of Delta Sigma Theta, had a line sister in the wedding who witnessed to me, but back then I was fresh off the burning sands and could not hear her witness. But it always stayed in the back of my mind. Why would she quit Delta?

The fact that the preacher who performed the ceremony was an Omega man made me think, forget that she's tripping. But I was the one who was really tripping; along with some of the other brothers from the wedding, we all drank brews in the basement of the church. I was very disrespectful to any organized religion.

Years later after studying all types of religions while pursuing my music career across the USA, my lifestyle began to catch up with me. I developed acute bronchitis. Also, the trips to the free health clinic for urinary tract infections were killing my immune system. I was dying. One night after coming home from the club—I prayed. I can't even remember what I said, but the prayer was sparked because I had a hangover from drinking. I woke up the next morning with the thought to fast off meat for thirty days and I obeyed.

What did I have to lose? About two weeks into this fast I stopped using drugs, stopped going to the strip clubs, and the desire to hit the stroll for hookers was gone too. Blaming it all on maturity, I went home for New Year's Eve headed to a New Year's Eve party, but I ended up in church and the message was clear. The minister preached about family and at the time I had no wife or children. I was 35 years old. Then things began to take off for me. I was soon on the road with several famous stars in a gospel play called Mama Dee's Girls. It felt good and I decided to do a gospel CD to balance out all the hardcore rap music that I was producing. Then I ended up at a church in Atlanta, Georgia. I did not have a Bible; in fact, I had not read the Bible in fifteen years, but one thing that I had was a testimony and I was telling everybody how free I was.

In the parking lot I heard a minister talking about doing something foolish while he was in college. I thought, what is he talking about? He then said that he was branded while in college. I went in after the sermon, walked up to him and saw that this preacher was a Q. I could see his brand through his shirt. I still wasn't ready to give up Omega or hear anything about my brands and tattoo. I just gave him my CD and left. After hearing my testimony, members of a church from New York asked me if I wanted to go to New York where they would take care of my room and board. They gave me my first Bible and about three months later after that I moved on from the church.

Even though I would read my Bible a little at first, day after day I grew stronger in the Word. Then one day after the Sept 11th bombing, I awoke on the couch speaking in tongues. Oh boy ... a couple weeks later I ended up at a revival where hands were laid on me at a Haitian church by a man from Nigeria.

There were many people in the back of the church praying when the revival minister's wife also began praying for me. Suddenly, I went flying into the air and landed head first on the hard cement ground. I thought my head was cracked open and bleeding. I struggled to get off the floor and after a few seconds was totally knocked out. Everyone was gone when I got up. I guessed it scared them or I might have been just lying there on the floor for a long time. All I know is that when I got up I knew to leave the church and go back to my Bible and really find out who this Jesus was. Little did I know that this would be the end of the life that I had grown accustomed to. After the revival I stayed at the Haitian church. God was up to something and I was not going to leave New York without that something.

One day while sitting and watching a pastor do a video show I noticed a man doing sign language. He was a former freemason and after his show he spoke to me outside and told me what our frats were founded upon—and it was not upon JESUS. I researched and prayed; two weeks later I was taking the Omega Psi Phi Fraternity license plates off my truck. This part may be hard for others to imagine, considering my loyalty to the organization, but it is true. After praying and reading the Bible for several weeks in a shoddy basement apartment in Hollis Queens with no television, but plenty friends (cockroaches and a rat), one Sunday morning as I was

getting ready for Sunday School, I heard a Voice come out of nowhere. I knew whose voice it was and began holding a conversation. He said the same thing three times: "Ask her to marry you."

The Voice was speaking of a Sunday school teacher at the church. I really didn't know this woman long, but that's what I heard the Voice say. I finally obeyed and 16 years later we are happily married with 9 children. I recalled the sermon about family New Year's Eve 2001, and one year later I would be married: February 8, 2002.

I used to sing a song that goes like this: I know I've been changed; Omega Psi Phi done signed my name. I was Q Psi Phi 'till the day I die. Well, my brothers and sisters, I died and was born anew. It happened to me and it can happen to you. Now I sing the same song, but the only difference is that I now sing it how it was originally written:

I know I've been changed; an Angel in Heaven done signed my name.

In the name of Jesus, I pray this testimony touches the heart of someone who is lost. I do this not because I am mad, I do this because God picked me up, turned me around, and placed my feet on solid ground. To the children of the Most High, remember, even when your Father disciplines and corrects you, He still loves you (Hebrews 12:7). In remembrance of what happened to the Apostle Paul, I was knocked down on my way to Damascus. A former member of Delta Sigma Theta sowed a seed in me in 1992 that took nine years to spring out of my soil. My prayer is that this seed will be planted into the hearts of others and be ready for the soon to come harvest, in the name of Yahshua.

The Home by the Sea 2010... During My Third year as a Dorm Director at Hampton University I needed a Grad Asst....On day a young man walked in my office and told me That he was about to start Grad School and needed a place to stay. I told him about The Grad Asst program and walked him over to Dean Hopewell's office, He was hired on the Spot ...When we went back to the dorm we chopped it up and he talked about his experience pledging Q @ South Carolina State ...Well I put a Purple and Gold bible in His hand and He stood Frozen for several minutes, Then He began to talk about when he Came to college he went nowhere without his Bible. After he crossed the Burning Sands the Bible was dropped off and he did not carry it again. Until I put it in His Hand, He carried the

Bible every day until I left Hampton University to pursue my next ministry TRIP .... Shalom to My Brother in Yahshua, Cedric ...

CONVICT US

Into the marvelous light that covers me Bright, as the son of righteousness from head to toe, I thank the God of Abraham Isaac and Jacob for creating my spirit body and soul. In a world of circumstances, I have fallen and cried aloud, but because you are a god of second chances I can now maintain a Christian lifestyle…. beyond this world of blood sweat and tears, we cling to the hope of glory but have only so many years to witness in joy and in pain… Broad is the way that leads to destruction and narrow is the way to paradise; the captain of my soul is the lord; Jesus Christ is the Master of my life.

After reading my testimony a young lady who I went to college with commented on what I had written:

Joe, you are one deep brother, sold out and bold enough to take a stand. I am so proud of what God has done through you and you know that he will reward your faithfulness. The revelation God has given you "is tight but it's right", I know what you are ministering is true...

I went through the battle of deciding whether to pledge at HU, I was newly spirit filled and growing in Christ, and prior to my experience with the power of God's Holy Ghost - I had my heart set to pledge... But I prayed about it "a lot" and the Lord intervened and sent someone to me who was a former soror for the organization I was going to pledge. She broke it down to me [about the real truth concerning Greek organizations] and I am so grateful [because this] topic is serious and controversial. A lot of "good" people have "pledged" their life to their organization of choice, but the Lord is so loving and awesome that he would never want us to be passive and accepting of something that is spiritually dangerous...

The bottom line is that he cares about our soul. I love you for caring enough to share your testimony and the truth with the people you care about. I hope that everyone who reads your insights will do so prayerfully and with a sincere heart...because only what we do for Christ will last when all of our earthly efforts and connections have faded away... Be blessed!!!! College Classmate

Delta DREAM

I was at Bishop TD Jakes' church when he took my hand, stretched forth my fingers, and yelled into my hand, "JESUS!!!" He looked out amongst the congregation and told them to bless me. As the people passed me, they would place in my hand cash and checks.

Several white people passed, and I was privy to their conversation. They commented that Bishop Jakes was a pimp. After they moved on a young lady approached me writing a check. When I glanced at her the second time, her Sunday attire had changed into Greek paraphernalia, and she was wearing Delta Sigma Theta paraphernalia from head to toe. I told her I had something to tell her and she was not going to like it. She backed up and said, "Don't tell me! I don't want to hear it!" I then began to share with her my testimony about my deliverance from Greek ritual associations. She handed me the check and walked away distraught.

I was on a message board 6 years ago and a young lady who was a member of Delta created a section called dreams, so I decided to post my dream on the message board. She read it and asked me to send it to a woman named Prophetess Lisa James. I agreed and sent it that night. I thought that she was not going to interpret the dream. I called a brother in the faith Minister Hatchett. While talking I said that she might be a delta and don't want to send me the interpretation. I decided to call her because her number was on her website. She picked up the phone and told me she had sent it a long time ago. It must have gone to my bulk mail, so she sent it again and gave me a number to call to make sure I received it. While on the phone with her I asked her, what did she think about the Lady delta in the dream…. She said that she pledged delta spr 92 the same year as me …I was like wow…. I asked her was she still a delta and she told me no. and that is how we met.

The State of the Black Greek Lettered Societies
1868 would mark the beginning of what we call Hampton University. Hampton University has always had a strong Christian heritage The Founder himself, Samuel Chapman Armstrong, was a son of missionaries in Hawaii. Even with this strong Christian heritage at Hampton somehow barbaric initiations became a part of Hampton Life. Hazing got to the point that States, Universities and organization would create anti-hazing policies and Laws. Two men were released from jail for hazing a young brother in Florida. And men and women have died while pledging.

If you join a black Greek lettered organization in America and don't go through an underground process you will be called a Paper member. These members can do official work for their organization but when it comes to the social aspect of most Black Greek Lettered Organizations, then so-called Paper members are disrespected, rejected and looked at by some members as imposters.

For a while I was a part of the problem and maybe the threat of jail could have made a difference in the way I initiated brothers into my organizations. But during the eighties we gave no thought to getting caught hazing or being hazed. But I will never forget the night a brother had an epileptic seizure while pledging. This would mark the end of my hardcore pledge tactics. And in 2001, when I began to follow Jesus Christ, that would mark the end of my days as a Hazer. To my fellow Christians,I pose a simple Question: Would Jesus Christ Pledge Your Organization?

Jesus Christ would never engage in illegal activity because He was sinless and would not violate His commandment, Thou shall not lie.

Would Jesus Christ join through the legal process?

He would not be a legitimate member either because He would never take the oaths. Jesus Christ said: —Swear not at all; neither by heaven; for it is God's throne: Nor by the earth; for it is his footstool: neither by Jerusalem; for it is the city of the great King. Neither shalt thou swear by thy head, because thou canst not make one hair white or black. But let your communication be, Yea, yea; Nay, nay: for whatsoever is more than these cometh of evil. —

Jesus Christ was hazed to the point of death and three days later rose from the dead. He is the Light of the World and if you follow Him you will become the light of the World. If you are a follower of Jesus, then His presence is in you. But you still must crucify your flesh daily. He loves you and I love you too. How good and pleasant it is for brethren to dwell together in unity.

Children, obey your parents in all things: for this is well pleasing unto the Lord.

Churchianity

Churchianity is a universal religion that speaks in an unknown Tongue called churchinese. In America, millions of people practice this religion. Most of the followers of this faith are sincere nice People who believe what they are doing on a routine basis is biblical. In addition, some of the followers of this faith are mean and nasty People who believe what they are doing on a routine basis is biblical. However, as you will see in this book the practitioners of churchianity are lost sheep and goats that are caught up in a labyrinth maze of traditions and rituals that are not based on the teaching and Commandments of our Lord and Savior Yahshua Ha Masheac.. Yahshua said

I am the way truth and the life no man comes to the Father but by Me. {John 14:6}

I am a dreamer and dream every night. Some things I remember and some I forget. Some are divine, and some are not, but I thank God for the Holy Ghost, wisdom and understanding concerning what I dream. My testimony is that God has spoken to me and I obeyed His specific instructions.

I have a personal relationship with Jesus Christ through revelations in the written word, dreams, and visions. As I stated earlier when I was at Bishop Eddie Long's Church and looked at a man I saw this man dressed like a hard pimp with rings on every finger. I first thought it was a drug flashback I looked away for a second and what I saw was gone...the man was in fact conservatively dressed in one ring on his hand. Time would reveal that everything I saw was real, but it was hidden from the natural man. What I have learned in my years on this planet is that God can reveal the heart and or mind of a man to another.

One day during a conversation with one of my rap partners he thought I was mad at the Pastor who was in that pimp vision. I told him I was not mad. Besides, if it hadn't been for him, I wouldn't have met my wife in New York City. But I did eventually leave the church. I attended several churches in NYC and I have concluded that most of those churches are not abusive cults. However, they tend to put so much trust in the personality and program of the leader of their organization that their ears are dull to the voice of the Good Shepherd, Yahshua.

One day while in Hollis Queens I remember looking across the room in my apartment and seeing a demon. My wife and I did not grab the kids and run out of the house like the movies. Instead, we fell to our knees in the living room and began to pray in the name of Jesus. And the spirit left.

Shortly after this encounter of the wicked kind my mom called and asked if I wanted to move into a house back in SC because my sister was moving out with her husband. My wife and I agreed so I left first to set things up and she would join me in a couple of months.

Upon returning to Hardeeville, SC, I fellowshipped with several ministries in the area. My father was a deacon in Savannah, Georgia at College Park Baptist Church. However, I knew I would not be going to that church because a couple years earlier I had left because the pastor did not agree with me about the freemason dedication block on the church building. But my wife was to join me in a couple weeks so I prayed and asked God to show me what church to attend. That night the pastor from College Park Baptist came walking up to me in a dream and told me to come with her to College Park. The next day I went and gave my offering. After the service she came up to me and asked if she could treat me to lunch. While at lunch the next day she informed me that she was also a member of a sorority and that she had denounced her membership. After which, she asked me to be the youth director at the church. I was sort of shocked, but I agreed, and we began to work together.

Soon after we began to work together, the church voted Pastor Lollis out. I had just preached my initial sermon, but I had not received my minister's license. Since she was out, me and my wife left and ended up in a predominately white congregation called Bluffton Assembly of God.

Pastor Scarborough was great. Fellowshipping with other brother and sisters in Yahshua outside of our own ethnicity and cultural comfort zones was a good experience. Daystar Ministry and Cry Savannah are two ministries where we would meet several fellow believers That came to Savannah from all over the country. Since I did not receive my ministry license every now and then I would think about when would I have my own church? One Sunday morning while sitting at The Lighthouse church in Ridgeland SC a woman preacher looked at me while she was preaching and said don't worry about being ordained by man because you have been ordained by God. A weight was lifted off me and till this day I no longer worried about when I would get my chance to lead a congregation. I enjoyed fellowship with the saints and future saints everywhere I went and was sent.

At Cry Savannah I met a brother named Phil who was the chaplain at the Ridgeland Correctional Facility where my sister worked, he invited me to the prison to talk to the inmates. I accepted right away because two years earlier I told some saints in New York that I would go with them to Rikers Island Prison and I did not go. About a month after not honoring my word, I was picked up by the Long Island City Police and taken to jail for driving with a suspended license.

My license was legit, but it was out of state and their computers were down. I spent the whole day in jail doing what I was supposed to do a couple of weeks earlier, which was ministering to our brothers in prison.

While taking care of my family I was enjoying working in the communities as a preacher of the Gospel of Yahshua. Then one-day Minister Gail Gray, an ex-member of a sorority, called me about a youth group at Savannah State University called Commissioned 2 Love. They were being suspended by the campus because of an accusation of harassment and hazing. Their style of ministering to frat members was different than mine but I decided to fellowship with them. I called Commissioned 2 love and was invited by the group leader to speak to the group. I spoke to them and then began to answer their questions. They asked me about Elder G Craig Lewis and The Truth Behind Hip Hop. I told them that I agreed with most of what he was saying but I did not agree on his approach with Gospel rap. But the reality was that I did not know much about the ministry to really speak on it.

I decided to look at EX Ministries and see what Elder G. Craig Lewis was talking about. I was led to read his vision and his message to Christian rappers, and I though both were right on the money. But after a few years I realized that he was not really in support of any Christian rappers publicly and after several attempts to contact him, I decided to see him in person. He dealt with much more than hip hop. I just chalked it up as a catchy title for his tapes to draw you in to hear all that he had to say. Then on his EX Cast he interviewed several Ex-black Greek ministers: Minister Melvin Jones (Pulpit Pimps website), Minister Fred Hatchett (dontgogreek.com website/Coming Apart at the Seams), and Minister Gail Gray (author of Offspring's of Abomination). I just knew that at some point Elder G Craig Lewis would hit me up because not only was I an EX BGLO member I also was a minister who did not use the term holy hip-hop. I referred to myself as a Gospel poet/rapper/singer. No contact was made.

I was puzzled so I decided to borrow the first video and look at the whole thing. The first Truth Behind Hip Hop video in a section toward the end of the tape, Brother Craig states that a demon asked him if he wanted to talk. Elder G Craig Lewis told the demon NO, and then he states that the Holy Spirit tells him to talk to the demon. I can't find an example of the Holy Spirit encouraging someone to entertain evil in the Bible. Believers must test all spirits, including any spirit that tells you to have a conversation with a demon.

That incidence was an exorcism with Kevin Thorton from the group Color Me Bad. Why run with the words of demons? They are just like their master, satan, and they are all LIARS. Many valid points have been made by Elder G Craig. The Truth behind Hip Hop is the Truth and the Lie behind Hip Hop is a Lie, each artist and song must be weighed individually. We should not have to choose sides between Elder G Craig Lewis and rap groups like Cross Movement because they cannot see eye to eye on every jot and jittle in scripture. Whose side am I on? I am own Yahshua's side. I deal with many artists who call themselves Hip Hop artists and one day we may be able to have one name for our music genre that everyone can agree on. But I will not go to war with brothers and sisters over the word hip hop. Buildings are not the church; real believers are and will continue to be the Body of the Messiah. If you are not part of the Body of Yahshua/Jesus, then you are simply a church goer and or an unbeliever. Through wisdom and discernment in Yah's Timing you will know who belongs to whom by their fruit.

22 But the fruit of the Spirit is love, joy, peace, longsuffering, gentleness, goodness, faith, 23 Meekness, temperance: against such there is no law. 24 And they that are Christ's have crucified the flesh with the affections and lusts. 25 If we live in the Spirit, let us also walk in the Spirit. Galations 5

The hip hop culture has rebellious and lawless spirit, but the phrase hip hop is not a demon. Demons are unclean foul spirits that are liars just like satan. Rap music like any other genre of music can be possessed by a holy or unholy spirit.

John 14:6 Yahshua saith unto him, I am the way, the truth, and the life: no man cometh unto the Father, but by me.

I know that we all make mistakes in ministry especially when dealing with deliverance ministry, I agree with Pastor G Craig on much of what he is doing. I have talked to several of his ministers for hours. Who knows one day we might chop it up. I did see him in three of my dreams.

And there was never a time in those dreams that I saw him as an agent of satan.

Pastor G. Craig Lewis and former President Obama Dream

Pastor G. Craig Lewis was preaching to a young audience in a theatre. President Obama and his wife were sitting alone in the balcony. The audience started turning towards President Obama. Pastor G. Craig became upset and told President Obama to tell them to turn back around and listen to Him. President Obama then stated that he had a problem with Pastor G. Craig Lewis....

My Thoughts on the dream ..A big part of Pastor G Craig Lewis audience is the so called black church in America. And a large portion of that church is in love with former President Obama. President Obama in the dream said that he has a problem with G Craig Lewis. That problem is that he is a champion of transgender homosexual and abortion rights. The very subjects that Pastor G Craig Lewis will not compromise on especially in the Church .

Minister Wes, a friend of mine in Savannah Ga., called me about a speaking engagement. I wanted to go and support him. When I stepped into the church I was approached by Pastor Marion he came up to me and began to prophesy. After church I went up to Pastor Marion and grabbed his wrists as though I had some handcuffs and asked him why when you fellowship with pastors that they instantly want to put some handcuffs on you. He just looked at me and I said that you must not be part of the church click in Savannah Ga. He said no I am not and in fact I am here to pull and bring out cutting edge ministries. I was like cool. Minister Irv was to speak at a hotel that evening and since he was the associate pastor, I decided to go hear him preach to get a better feel for this ministry. I had an appointment with another Nigerian preacher and a woman at a local restaurant. After our meeting we both proceeded to the hotel meeting room to hear Minister Irv preach. This meeting was being given by a woman called Mother Hines. She had moved away from Savannah but would come back to hold church services in Savannah. When Minister Irv preached, he came straight out of the Word with most of his time spent on reading the RED Letters(Jesus words). Then he concluded his message.

The way the meeting was set up afterwards people could ask the speaker questions and give comments on the ministry presentation. One man stated that Minister Irv did not give any solutions. I spoke and told him that he might not have heard the solution presented but after reading the words of Yahshua, he gave a clear solution. Then I repeated the solution. The solution was get out of these meetings and go into the streets. Mother Hines' followers also began to really criticize Pastor Marion over what he was doing in the city. I decided that I would fellowship with these brothers. Every Monday we would have leadership classes for the new ministry that Pastor Marion had started.

I drove from Hardeeville to the Deep South side of Savannah to attend. As I walked across the parking lot, I noticed in the pastor's parking place a truck with Alpha license plates. I decided just to observe as Pastor Marion and his Associate Pastor Dr. Irv began to teach. I knew that Minister Irv was the brother of Alpha Phi Alpha.

About a week later I approached Pastor Marion and explained to him why I denounced my membership and oath to the fraternity that I had pledged. I also told him about the outreach ministry that I conducted on Saturdays in Hardeeville this ministry was in a bar that was closed on Saturdays. He said that he knew the area well and that he would join me in my efforts to reach out to my community

Cross Da Traxxx. After three weeks of Monday classes Pastor asked me to speak to Minister Irv about his fraternity. I said I would when the time was right. I was building a relationship with Minister Irv. I did not want him to think that I came to take his position in Shield of Faith Ministry. I gave Pastor Marion a book by Minister Gail Gray called Offspring of Abomination.

While getting dressed one evening I knew that this day would be the day that I would share my testimony with Minister Irv. I wore my Biblical Perspective of Greekdom t-shirt. On the front were several ex-BGLO Ministers and on the back, were all the unofficial mascots of the black frats and sororities. I was sitting on the front row and Mr. Irv and his fiancée came in and she sat directly behind me and he sat directly in front of me. After the class I asked Minister Irv for a few minutes to talk to him. We sat in the back of the church and I showed him my brand. He was happy at first because he thought that the ministry had just received a fellow Greek member. I proceeded to tell him my testimony and he went into serious thought and asked me to come outside. Before I could share anything else with him, he began to prophesy and speak the very things I was about to say to him. Then he repented, asked forgiveness from God and denounced on the spot. A minute later he pulled the license plate off his car. We walked back into the church and he went to the front and slammed the plate on the floor.

I was like wow and Pastor Marion began to share with me that because of Minister Irv he was about to join the grad chapter. A week or so later internal and financial problems began to surface, and Pastor Marion lost the million-dollar church building, so he started having services in the meeting rooms of a hotel. I told Minister

Irv about Commissioned 2 love Ministry and one day we both showed up at the church. He eventually began to participate in the Biblical Perspective of Greekdom Conferences.

Hampton Savannah Connection

As a teenager I went to junior high and high school in Hampton Va. and Savannah Ga. My Father graduated from Savannah State University in 1972 and I graduated from Hampton University in 1989.I worked at Hampton University for several years and briefly worked at Savannah State University in 2002.

On November 17, 2007 I was asked to minister to the students of Hampton University about biblical perspective of greekdom. This is where I met Minister Cullen. He was the advisor of the Student Christian Association at Hampton University. The Conference was awesome and afterwards I felt the need to move back to Va. I did not know how or when, but I knew that I would be in Hampton Va. Preaching the Gospel of Jesus Christ.

During the Spring semester of 2008 I was asked by Sister Larinda, The President of Commissioned 2 Love, if I would participate in the play Trapped with Minister Wes.

Hampton University's Student Christian Association would be at the dress rehearsal in Savannah Ga. After the play, I spoke with Minister Cullen after hearing that he was a residential hall director. I had told my wife a couple of months or so earlier that I had to become a Residential Hall Director so that I could go back to school and handle several of my ministry projects. A month later, I would be working at Hampton University as a Dorm Director in training. I sold everything I owned, leaving our big four-bedroom home in the country and moved into a hotel room on campus. I was launching out into the deep and letting my faith take me somewhere that I had never been in Yahshua/Jesus.

Commission 2 Love wanted me to come to Florida A&M University for the Biblical Perspective of Greekdom and to play the role in the Gospel Play Trapped. The Play had become to carnal and because of arguing with campus officials on the second showing we were not allowed to hold the Biblical Perspective of Greekdom Conference the next day on the campus. When I got home I went to work on making music for the play that I thought would be more appropriate for a Gospel Play.

Then I called another minister who was with us in Florida for writing a review of the play so that when it came back to Savannah State it would be on point. Out of nowhere I was informed that the leader of Commissioned 2 love Larinda and Chris were going to get married. This was a shock to me because I was under the impression that Chris was engaged to someone else a recent graduate of Hampton University and Larinda was going to marry another brother. I called them from Va. To challenge them on their timing and how they were treating the young lady who was engaged to Chris. I was told that I only knew half the story. Brother Chris told me he could show me in the scriptures why this was going to happen. I told Chris instead of going to New York for the winter break at Hampton University I was coming to Savannah Ga.

We tried to work things out, but it was over. those young people had fallen into the trap of worshipping their pastor. And the pastor allowed them to worship her. Many leaders call this honoring their leadership. Now everyone from outside the group were being led by demons if they disagreed with the ministry. My Ministry partner Fred Hatchett said we just saw the formation of a cult. Minister Fred Hatchett is one of the first ministers to have written a book about Black college secret societies. His book is called Coming Apart at the Seams.

Even though I moved to Virginia in the summer of 2008 I kept in contact with Minister Irv by phone. On June 10, 2009, Brother Irv called me and told me that he bumped into Brother Chris. He said that Chris told him that he had to talk to Brother Phil. That was weird because they had my contact information.

He gave Irv his new number and asked him to ask me to call him. Even though we had not talked since Nov.-Dec 2008, I still called him up. I talked to Brother Chris for just a second and then he passed the phone to Larinda his wife. She spoke with me for a good while. When I asked to speak to her husband again, he would not speak to me. I began to speak to everybody. I did not know we were on speaker phone. It was dead quiet on the phone, I told several members that I loved them and to remember that I had never lied to any of them or acted out of order with any of the young ladies in the ministry. Then my cell phone died. The next day I met several male members on the Savannah State campus who thought I'd hung up on them. I informed them `that my cell phone charge went out. One young guy asked me where have I been and why I have not come around C2L in Savannah. I looked at this new member and informed him that I moved to Hampton Va. a year ago.

Saints, I strongly urge you to wait and be patient for your spouse. I thank God I met my wife at the age of 35 and got a chance to see and raise my children. Ladies, wait for that man and fellas stay in that Word so that when she comes across your path, you will know that this is your wife.

Me and my brother Chris never met in Savannah Ga. I went back to Va. and had this dream.

Divination Dream

I was in the room with a lady who was sitting on a couch staring at a colorful crystal ball like object on the coffee table. Another man and woman were in the room with me watching her stare at the object in a trance like state. I turned to the Lady and asked her what that object was. She did not want to tell me and suddenly without opening her mouth, the word divination came out one letter at a time. I read the word when it was completely out of her face Instantly, all three of us headed for the door. I was first and when I grabbed the door knob I did not go out because a young man was lying at the foot of the door. He got up and I asked him, "What are you doing here?" He replied, "I came to learn." I said, "Learn about what?" "Demons!" He then proceeded to follow me and the other two people out of the door. As soon as we got outside the Lady followed, trying to fight. But we resisted her and kept moving. The young man followed me back home to Hampton University. A car pulled up to him loaded with people and they seduced him back into the car. I went into my dormitory where the fire alarm had just gone off. I handled my dorm business and woke up.

At first, I did not know exactly what the meaning of the dream was. One day I was going into my Dormitory apartment and TBN was on. Karen Wheaton was singing and as I watched and enjoyed the worship and praise music suddenly I felt The Holy spirit begin to move like a mighty wind around my body. It went from the soles of my feet to the top of my head and when it stopped. I had the interpretation of my dream.

That Spirit of divination was operating through Larinda and the young man on the floor was Chris. The people who followed me out the door were my fellow ministers who were called to help this ministry. My Prayer is that the Ministry leaders repent and are being led by the Holy Spirit of YHVH in the name of Yahshua.

Lost and Found Village Story ..Part 1

The year was 1975 when Janice was born. She was her parents' only child; even though they were Christians, they did not go to church or read the Bible. Janice's dad had a good job and her mom worked part-time at the elementary school. Her childhood was a normal one, and like most American Christian families they celebrated Easter, Halloween, the 4th of July and Christmas. One Christmas morning in 1987; Janice received a gift that would change her whole life. Under the neatly decorated tree were several gifts. She quickly unwrapped them all. A particular gift stood out. It was called Ouija Board.

She took it to her room and began to play. After several weeks of Janice attempting to make the board answer her questions, a voice started to speak to her. At first, she was nervous, but the voice was very friendly and gentle. The voice told Janice that she was a spirit sent to guide and teach her. But Janice was still uneasy and decided to throw away the Ouija Board. And as a young child she did not hear that voice again.

Several years went by and Janice went off to a historical black college. She had not seen that many black people in one area in her whole life. It was a very powerful experience for her; Her freshman year consisted of going to class, relaxing in the dorms and partying every weekend, which begins on Thirsty Thursday—a day dedicated to drinking to initiate the weekend festivities. After all the partying was done, Sunday morning at 11:00 am, everyone was in the Chapel receiving prayer for their hangovers.

One Saturday, Janice decided to go to a party in the apartments located directly across the street from the college campus. Everything was fine until Janice made a crucial mistake by leaving her red cup on the dining room table. When she came back, her drink was still there, and she continued to sip on the fruity beverage.

After she finished her cup, she found herself in the living room dancing to some intoxicating hip hop music. Unbeknownst to Janice, while she'd been in the bathroom earlier, someone had slipped something in her cup, which caused her to pass out in the middle of the apartment. She woke up in the emergency room.

A young lady named Sarah sat with her at the hospital. Sarah was a resident assistant at her dormitory and was also a member of the Student Christian Association. Sarah had a long conversation with Janice about how dangerous her lifestyle was, which could lead to spiritual and physical death. Janice was very captivated by the conversation and asked Sarah, "What is spiritual death?" Sarah began to share with Janice and told her that she would better understand if she came with her to the Student Christian Association meetings.

While lying in a hospital bed, Janice had plenty of time to think about her life and concluded that she needed to make a change; she was eagerly looking forward to the

Student Christian Association meeting. When the day finally came, she was the first one in the place. After a couple of hours of praise and worship, she looked around and realized that it wasn't an official University meeting, but a Bible study campus ministry meeting sponsored by a word of process church. In the beginning, it was all love with plenty of hugs, smiles and kisses. Everybody was so happy, and the music was something that she had never heard before. The whole meeting was very emotional, and it felt like everybody was in some sort of trance.

After everybody settled down, the leader of the Bible study began to share with the group a very personal testimony and afterwards he asked the audience if there was anyone among them who had gone through a similar experience. Everybody began to reveal their darkest, deepest and most intimate thoughts, including Janice. To her, it was like some type of therapy session. Janice was hooked. She was present every time the doors of the church were opened, and her new friends were all members of the word of process church. She was assigned a mentor to make sure that she was trained properly. Janice joined the usher battalion and the dynamic Gospel choir; she also took a part time job so that she could participate in giving to the church and the pastor.

Her grades began to slip, and she rarely called home. She finally did get a chance to talk to her parents and she told them that she would not be able to come home for the holidays because she had to perform in a Christmas play at the church as a singing High- priestess. While talking to her father she mentioned how wonderful her church daddy was. Her father screamed over the phone and told her that she had only one Daddy and that was him and she only had one heavenly Father and that was God. According to him, the pastor was just there to help, equip and train her in her spiritual walk.

While in her apartment, Janice thought about her conversation with her father and she thought that there was nothing wrong with her calling the pastor "Daddy". But she was still puzzled by the fact that her father was so mad. She blocked it out of her mind because she had to concentrate on the Christmas play, which was supposed to be different this year. It was going to be a mixture of African traditions and the wizard of Oz. The name of the play was The Wizard and the Village. The Pastor decided that they needed something fresh and exciting for this winter season. He kept a Nativity scene with the three maji and baby Jesus in the lobby of the church right next to the Christmas tree; Janice felt so blessed to be a part of the play. The Wizard and the Village play practice was held every night. It was very draining. The director of the play wanted them to really get into their roles. She did not want them to come out of character even after rehearsal was over. Janice didn't really agree with that because she was a high-priestess and did not want to be acting like a high-priestess all day and night. That's when she started to question what was really going on at this church.

Janice decided that she needed to set up a meeting between her and the director of the play. At the meeting, she asked the director why she felt that the actors needed to stay in character 24/7; the director thought that Janice was being rebellious. The director tried to explain the importance of the screenplay. The director finally told her to go home and read the play again. Janice decided to give the play one more chance. She went back to her apartment, pulled out the manuscript and read the manuscript from cover to cover.

The Wizard and the Village Play

One day, Danielle was walking down a dusty dirt road in Carolina and she heard this loud noise coming from the woods. As she got closer, she realized that it was some type of religious ceremony inside a building. She eased up to the window to see what was going on inside; she saw some people drinking out of jars and others were holding snakes in their hands.

She was very intrigued. She decided to go in. At first it was as though nobody knew she was there. She had never seen anything like this before in her life. She grew up with her uncle and aunt and they were not that religious. When they did go to church it was rather boring in her opinion. Finally, the leader asked her to come down front. Before she knew it, Danielle was laid out on her back. When Danielle woke up she was no longer in what she considered Carolina. The place looked like the movie Roots, a Movie about African American Slavery. And she was surrounded by a strange looking group of people. They were singing but she did not recognize the language. One of the men began to speak to her in English. He said that she had a strong root on her. She was puzzled. The last thing Danielle remembered was being in a church. The man said every church is not a church...

The place was an African village located in South Carolina at first Danielle was nervous but was led and trained by an older woman from the village. The Older woman who was a High priestess told Danielle that to get back home she would have to consult the Wizard of the Village. The High priestess taught Danielle the art of divination and she became one of the best tarot card readers in the village. The Village had become a tourist attraction in South Carolina. People would come from all over the world and pay good money to the best fortune tellers. Soon the wizard began to take notice of Danielle because of her gift. The High Priestess informed Danielle that she was to become the Wizards next wife. Danielle cried and cried because she wanted to go home and knew that if she became the wizard's wife she would never leave the village.

One day a tourist came through the village his name was Immanuel. She met him at the well while drawing water for dinner. He asked her why she was sad. Danielle for some reason confided that she was a Christian but somehow ended up in the village and did not know how to get back home. Immanuel prayed for Danielle at the well and the spirit of divination was cast out of her and she was filled with the spirit of Jesus Christ. Immanuel disappeared and immediately the wizard and High priestess showed up. They knew Danielle was changed and kicked her out of the village because they knew if she stayed the Spirit of Jesus would spread like the flu.

Danielle was publicly beaten to set an example for the rest of the village. She passed out and when she woke up she was back in the church with the snakes. She got up off the floor ran outside as she slowed down and began to walk and think about the events that took place Immanuel appeared again to her and told her ...

"Heaven can be entered only through the narrow gate! The highway to hell is broad, and its gate is wide enough for all the multitudes who choose its easy way. But the Gateway to Life is small, and the road is narrow, and only a few ever find it.

Matthew 7:13-14

Even though Janice loved the play and thought it was very creative she felt the 24/7 role playing was too much so after meditating and praying about the play, Janice decided to come out from among them and separated herself from the Word of Process Church ...... **Part 2 coming soon**

I Understand(Rhyme)

A sinner with no remorse behold a pale horse my bible was rap pages the magazine was the source as I walked on the dark side of the force Star Wars My heroes were obi won kanobi and yoda of course

I'm in the psychic eye my alibi was playing tarot cards the skill can be attained with spades diamond and hearts my residence is clubs I pay plenty tithes at the door no going broke at the bar we are hitting the liquor store

Manipulating mental with medulla gymnastics invisible pimp game laced with blind tricks gets drastic it's tragic how the magic is not done by traditional magician's divination is witchcraft fronting as feminine intuition those demons got cast out then I hit the floor

What did you ask me? why I don't play spades and bid wiz anymore?

Black female Greek Business Testimony

I pledged a Sorority over 34 years ago. I have a business where suddenly, I can make thousands and thousands (maybe even millions) of dollars recreating Greek and Masonic memorabilia. I am convicted. I was very young when I knelt on my knees and took the oath.

I did not discern the eternal damnation I was facing by giving in to the extremely seductive idol worship and false sisterhood. I say false because it is not built upon the rock of Christ. The Holy Word tells us clearly; covers this topic regarding false gods and taking oaths.

At the end of this life, I want to stand in front of my Judge and be counted among His flock. Why did we pledge our lives to an entity that did not GIVE us life? Greek organizations are under an agenda that reaches far back in history way before the college frats and sororities. We are deaf, blind and arrogant.

I feel sad for those who have ears and will not hear; eyes and will not see, until it is too late. As it is, the deprogramming we must go through is not easy. We all truly seek love through brotherhood and sisterhood. May God bless all who are in search of truth and forgiveness from the Lord; true enlightenment

5040 and Go Go ...2009

At this Point I have settled in a Dorm Director at my Alma Mata Hampton University. I went to have my pants Tailored early one Saturday morning. There was another man in the shop, we began talking and soon realized that we knew the same people. We were both gospel artist and after about an hour of fellowship we exchanged phone numbers. The gentlemen name was Derek and I received a call from him two weeks later. He said that the president of my band has just joined that same fraternity I was in. I told Derrick to put the young man on the phone, after speaking briefly not only was he a member of Omega but he also was a part of the local chapter I had come through in 1992.

I told him forget the phone conversation give me the directions I'm on my way. I meet Derrick and Go Go George at their band practice. They played gospel music with a gogo swing, we instantly hit it off. He was a husband a father and had a genuine love for Jesus Christ.

Regardless of our fraternity affiliation we were Brothers in Yahshua. A couple weeks later there was a rap event at Virginia Beach at Mount Trashmore, it was sponsored by a young ministry called BeChurch Unusual aka as the 50-40.

I met the pastor of the church in a field while watching Scott Lane perform on stage. I told him that I knew one of his ministry partners C.J. Blaire out of the Washington D.C. area. He then informed me that C.J. Blaire would be preaching in the morning at the fifty-forty. I told pastor Q that I would be there in the morning. The next day I drove to Virginia Beach and sat at the back of the church, I thought to myself that C.J. Blaire was not coming, but just like that , he was stepping into the fifty-forty. After C.J.Blaire preached I went down to the front to meet him. I told him if he needed me to come and preach in the D.C. area about secret societies in the church I would come and break it down. Pastor Q heard what I said and pulled me to the side, and that was when we both realized that we had crossed the burning sands into omega land. I never thought about pastor Q's name because his name was Quentin.

For the next two and a half years I was able to fellowship with three brothers Derrick, George, Cedric, Quentin and many other brothers and sisters on a regular basis. My fellowship in Hampton would end abruptly because my family would once again be expanding, and I could no longer stay in the dormitory with that many children, and on another note the campus was becoming more ecumenical. My last email from my boss would say that dorm directors could no longer instruct bible studies. When I checked the number of the email, it was email number 666. An example of how ecumenical the campus was becoming that winter they would have an interfaith Christmas party. These things added up to me knowing that my season in Virginia as a dorm director at Hampton University was up. We put our stuff in storage, packed the family and headed back to Hardeeville South Carolina. In the next five years God would add three more children into our family making it a total of eight children. When my wife became pregnant with our ninth child we agreed to move to Houston Texas.

President Harvey meets Brother P Dream

While working at Hampton University I had a Dream. I was standing in Presidents Harvey's kitchen. At first there was no problem and he asked me to go into the Basement. When I turned towards the basement I could see what was in the basement.The Basement was filled with unclean foul corruption. It reminded me of a dream That I had about hell. In that dream about hell I could not believe I was there. I was desperately trying to GET OUT. I thought, jumping in this nasty river was the way out and that's when I heard a voice say if you jump in that nasty river you will never make it out. Well just like that dream I knew not to go into that crazy basement. I told President Harvey no. He was very upset and then commanded that I go into the basement. Once again, I said no. He turned around still mad and walked away. I then walked upstairs in his house went into his dresser drawer and took his wallet. I opened the wallet and took out several bills. And that's how that dream ended

University Revival Rhyme

Here is an open letter to the graveyard full of dead man's bones, son of man prophecy liars present sweet words that melt like ice cream cones. Cellar digital phones with data plans will transmit this Rit ,I spit rhymes dipped in the blood of the Passover lamb with the power of the son who is the great I am ,College clergy bound up by the rules of the elite who want you to kiss their ring when they should be washing your feet ween them of the milk and increase the meat please don't get lost in the beat.

Secular scholars, collars for dollars, holler from manmade thrones steeples and cathedrals that originate from Rome with gothic designs human jellyfish with no spines whispering hissing snakes in the grass house of glass with another Christ to mass

The chief cornerstone the rock that will break up the foolishness with no backstage pass only what you do for Yahushua would last double minded blind reprobate and delusional from one yard to the next the suspects are unusual

Haters love to flex while strange flesh intersect committing crimes against nature children of disobedience try to rape you adulterers fornicating administrators want to date you

Wicked ones promoting with their nose in the sky don't ask why unless you want to hear a lie this old man got to die and be Born Again... the man who picks up trash is treated like trash if you got the position and cash you don't even have to ask

While the trash man begs for scraps from the masters table end the end we know YHVH is able to provide all your needs but today I rebuke university lust and greed we know gods speed take heed

From a messenger who knows the deal I'm going to step out on faith Yahshua take the wheel broken hearts can heal thou shall not murder thou shall not steal.

No graven images of gods compare to that which is true, love YHVH and your neighbor then let it do what it do.

Eat this bitter from Facebook Instagram to twitter I spent three years underground in the cut a heavy hitter no fear here as you read you will begin to shake and quiver a punch from my gut straight to your kidneys and your liver guess who coming to dinner

I stepped into your house and you weren't surprised frustration sat in cause Yah made me wise you made a deal with the beast called compromise

I'm a sheep in wolf's clothing sent for the lost my daddy told me a long time ago to count the cost these souls are more precious than diamonds and pearls Satan is on the yard eating boys and girls Whoa be unto the inhabitants of this world

Heaven is missing an angel the adversary is on the ground these unclean spirits that control the systems are foul I know a physician who is skilled in circumcisions We wrestled not against flesh and blood this is a spiritual mission

The Real H.U. revival has begun the separation of children of the most Yah from the children of the sun.

The Son of Man Returns Dream

As I was looking into the night sky I observed a star falling. Then another fell and all of them began to fall. They were falling into the formation of a man. As soon as all them were in position the Man turned and his leg stepped towards the earth. I said in the Dream. That's It! No More decisions to follow Christ! He is coming Right Now! When I woke up I just thought about what I just saw. Like Wow …. Then one day while reading Matthew 24 again these words just jumped off the page.

*Immediately after the tribulation of those days shall the sun be darkened, and the moon shall not give her light, and the stars shall fall from heaven, and the powers of the heavens shall be shaken: And then shall appear the sign of the Son of man in heaven: and then shall all the tribes of the earth mourn, and they shall see the Son of man coming in the clouds of heaven with power and great glory. And he shall send his angels with a great sound of a trumpet, and they shall gather together his elect from the four winds, from one end of heaven to the other. **Matthew 24***

I had read this several times but this time I was reading my dream and it gave me a greater sense of urgency to share the good news about the love of Yahshua with the saints and future saints. Unity of faith will not come through the current church system. That will continue to fight and split over silly matters...it will come through the Holy Spirit bypassing the carnal will of men and women...the Roman Catholic Church has the right concept with the ecumenical movement. Bringing all the orgs under an umbrella of interfaith love and getalongedness...it's just that little part about that manmade Priest system that does not sit well with those who are filled with the Spirit of Truth ...Melchizedek Priesthood rising Worldwide a poem by Brother P

Stop Playing Open Vision

An Open Vision is seeing something while awake. One day while sitting am older black man appeared. He looked at me and said Stop Playing !

We Will Cut You

(A Barber Shop Story)

CHARACTERS James - Shop Owner Don - James' Friend Fred - Barber Foquan - Local Sherrod - Barber Ali - Shop Hannibal - Quartet Bum 1 Guitarist Rapper Stranger

This story takes place in a barber shop. It shows how black people truly interact with each other. The first scene opens with a barber shop quartet singing a traditional song with that soul flavor.

James: Now that's some good music. Young people should listen to more of this stuff. Maybe they'll stop killing each other.

Ali: Music doesn't cause people to kill each other. Poor moral values are the cause of people killing each other.

James: Well, it won't be too much more foolishness with this 3 strikes and you're out.

Don: It should be one strike and you're out. An eye for an eye, tooth for a tooth. That's what I'm talking about. Real justice.

Sherrod: Are you trying to say that if I rape your daughter, I should get raped?

Don: No, no son. I say rape equals death! Child molestation equals death. Armed robbery equals death. Death equals death. That's what I'm saying.

Fred: You a hard man!

Don: I'm no different from any other man!

James: How do you figure?

Don: If someone raped your daughter, you would want to kill them and Fred, if someone killed you wife - death would be your sentence. So be truthful. Think of your own family when making decisions.

Fred: Well, how about if the rapist was your son?

Don: Then my son deserves to die.

James: Would you make homosexuality a crime?

Don: Yeah, no question. James: How would you punish them?

Don: Death . . . no I'm just joking. I don't know how I would deal with that.

Fred: If my son was gay, I would die. I don't even like to think about it.

Foquan: Why would it hurt you?

Fred: Why? Because I want grandchildren to play with when I'm old. Two men can't make no babies; just AIDS.

Foquan: That's not true.

Fred: Well, why do so many gay men die of the disease, that's the research I want done. Even lesbians don't get it like the men get it. Somethings going on.

James: I guess you have to be safe in 1994 and rubbers isn't safe enough. You boys just say no until you get married!

All the boys: Mr. Odom, you are bugging (in unison).

James: No, I'm not bugging!

As he talks to the boys, an accident happens outside. Everyone runs out to see it. They slowly come back into the shop.

Hannibal: Man, did you see the way that bicycle was wrapped around his leg?

Foquan: Yeah. Boy, he's pretty messed up. I wonder if they're ever going to catch the guy who hit him?

James: Do you remember the time that guy hit that boy and didn't stop because he was scared?

Don: Yeah. I remember. The guy was Jewish. I think he did the right thing by not stopping.

Fred: Man, you're crazy!

Don: Just imagine, he probably was thinking about that boy who got beat down in L.A. when he stopped that 18-wheeler tractor/trailer.

James: Yeah, the Reginald Denny incident was unfortunate.

Foquan: Those rioters would not have stopped me on roller skates!!!

James: Why are people so scared?

Fred: Well, James - are you trying to say you're not afraid? You know, sometimes in these inner city, crack infested neighborhoods . . .

James: Yeah, though I walk through the valley of the shadow of death, I will fear no evil; for thou art with me.

Don: I hope thou - is a gun because that's the only things these hoodlums understand.

Sherrod: You have a point there.

James: Guns are not the answer. You must have a little faith anyway. If you look for trouble, you are going to find it.

Bum 1: Hey, hey - can anybody spare a dime or two - for some coffee and doughnuts?

Don: You have the wrong shop! The Police Precinct is down two blocks! *Everybody laughs!*

Bum 1: How about you, sir? Can I borrow some change?

James: Listen, son. You must pull yourself up by the bootstraps. Now here is a New Testament. Eat up them words. They will fill you up. Alright Everybody! Get Out! Time to close the shop. Foquan, go see what them boys are up to outside!

Everyone outside is listening to the boy's rap to the beat box (human sounds). The next morning James arrives at the barber shop to discover an old raggedy man with a guitar standing outside in the rain.

Old Man: Excuse me, Mister. Can I come inside and play my guitar for donations? I won't take up any space.

James: Hey! I wish I could help, but we don't allow people to solicit our customers. Sorry.

Old Man: I won't bother your customers. They'll love my music.

James: Nope, nope, nope. Sorry. I can't help you. There is a shelter 5 blocks down the street. Go play for the homeless.

Old Man: I do that all the time because I am homeless, Mister.

James: Well, here is a New Testament. Read up on that home in the sky where rent is never due - and maybe those words will change your life.

Old Man: Alright. Thank you, James for the Bible. I'll be seeing you. Before the old man leaves he sits outside the shop in the rain and sings a song.

(The same day, later in the afternoon.)

James: Fred, you should have heard this old man outside my shop this morning. He had the voice of an angel. I was shocked!

Fred: Yeah, you can't judge a book by its cover

Don: Fred, you are right on that because even though I am big black and ugly as ever. I am the man with the ladies!

James: Later for all those tall tales. You see, those young girls - they look like grown women. When we were young, girls were not so developed.

Fred: Ah, silky, silky-uhm uhm. The temptation is getting stronger and like the late great Marvin Gaye said, when I get that feeling I need healing.

James: You better chill out before you get one of those STDs! The price of sin is death.

Don: I think it's the milk and all of the growth hormones they give the cows.

Fred: It's got to be something!

James: Those hormones must be affecting grown women, too. It's like being married is a competition.

Fred: I know. Women have money now and with money comes power. They have money and power but have yet to accept their responsibilities.

Don: What responsibility?

Fred: If a woman goes on a date, she pays if she makes more money - or at least half of the bill.

James: But you know, that's not going to happen. Women want you to open the door, protect them, and show them a good time. At the same time, they want E-R-A. Could you imagine your daughter getting drafted in the Marines and becoming a P.O.W.? No way!

Don: The divorce rate is so high because women want to wear the pants and men aren't willing to give them up well most men!

Fred: The same thing is happening with the races. Blacks want power. Whites don't want to give it up, so just like women you have to take cause nobody in their right mind is going to give it away.

Don: A power struggle. But no matter, I love women - especially black women.

James: Why do you love black women?

Don: Because black women in America are strong, independent and come in every shade, color, and size. Sisters go from the whitest of whites to the blackest of blacks, and it's all good.

James: You are a black racist (laughing)

Don: Call it what you want. James what color is your wife?

James: black Don: exactly

The quartet comes in and sings another song. "Pretty Brown Eyes". The next morning James comes into the shop and finds that his door has been tampered with...

James: Listen Don, someone tried to break into my place last night. The lock was scraped up. It was probably those hoodlums who were out there rapping.

Don: Why don't these young kids join the nation of Islam or something?

Fred: That Louis Farrakhan knows exactly what those young boys need.

James: What they need is Jesus!

Don: Christians have forgotten that discipline is the best gift you could give a child.

Fred: Spare the rod and ruin the child is what the Bible says. The government doesn't want you to punish you own children, but they're quick to throw their butts in jail.

Don: When Martin was alive, black Christians were not afraid to take to the streets. You Christians have integrated and gotten comfortable; scared to lose the stuff you've accumulated.

Fred: The nation is willing to put it on the line for her people. Those black Muslims are hungry for equality, justice, and power - and the best part about it is they know we can do it without handouts.

James: Well, why don't you guys come to church with me tomorrow to get the fire started?

Don: You can go to church or you can go to the mosque; but tonight, I'm going to the all-night rump shaker contest. I'll be sleep by tomorrow morning.

Fred: I'm taking my family to the Amusement Park Sunday, so no church for the kid.

A young man dressed like in very urban gear comes in the shop.

James: May I help you, young man?

Rapper: Yeah, check it out. I want to do some work with your church choir. I heard they could blow and I wrote a song for a powerful choir!

James: I'm sure it's good, son, but we don't allow rap in our church. That's the devil's music.

Rapper: The devil! For real I am out!

Don: What are you talking about, the devil's music?!

Fred: Yeah, it's not the music, but the message in the music.

James: I don't want to hear it. "No Rap" at the African Methodist Church of Jesus Christ! Not ever!

Don: James, open your eyes. What do you call it when black preachers preach, and the choir starts hooping hollering moaning, and groaning then the drummer starts drumming; can I get a witness?

Fred: Yes!

Don: Can I get an Amen?

 Fred: Amen.

Don: that ain't nothing but rap! Christian rap!

James: No rap. Now, let's close this shop so I can get some rest and go to church in the morning.

SUNDAY MORNING In the middle of the service, a man came in and the congregation fell to their knees. Everyone except James.

James: Who are you?

Stranger: I am the Lord.

James: If you are the Lord, why didn't I know like the others?

Jesus: It's no surprise that you don't know me. I came to you three times and you turned me away each time. I was hungry, and you gave me no food and drink. I was cold and wet, and you gave me no shelter. When I came to spread the word to your congregation through the choir, you would not allow me to. As you turned your back on all those who needed your help, I must do the same now.

Mat 25:40 And the King shall answer and say unto them, Verily I say unto you, In as much as ye have done it unto one of the least of these my brethren, ye have done it unto me.

9000 Sermon

For years i heard that Jesus fed 5000 with 5 loaves of bread and two fish. And then i read the bible myself and learned that this was just part of a bigger story. Yes, he did feed 5000 and after that miracle he walked on water and performed several more supernatural acts. He then fed 4000 more people with 7 loaves of bread and a few fish.

And the story continues with them travelling on a boat and Jesus told them to beware of the leaven of the Pharisees and Herod. They thought he was mad because they had no bread, but the Leaven was corruption and hypocrisy. Jesus then begins to remind them of the two-miraculous feeding of the 9000 people.

And when Jesus knew it, he saith unto them, why reason ye, because ye have no bread? perceive ye not yet, neither understand? have ye your heart yet hardened? Having eyes, see ye not? and having ears, hear ye not? and do ye not remember? When I brake the five loaves among five thousand, how many baskets full of fragments took ye up? They say unto him, Twelve. And when the seven among four thousand, how many baskets full of fragments took ye up? And they said, Seven. And he said unto them, how is it that ye do not understand? Mark 8

Jesus is the Bread of Life and when he is present all things are possible.

Impossible (song)

There is nothing impossible for my God. He moves mountains by faith he will mend a broken heart ...There is nothing that my God can't do He is the creator and he came just for you. My God is the Joy and the strength of My Life ...Come out of darkness into the Marvelous Light. Is it Possible for young people to serve the Lord texting in the church pews oh so bored Could it be that it was simple back then or is that the traditions of men...never was the answer to sin ..We busy 106 and parking Thirsty women barking A whole generation never taught about Noah's Ark and on top of all that the good life is Oh so elusive Blood Fathers are ghost spiritual fathers are abusive But My God can mend a broken heart Set the captive free The Word of God is smart His Blood was shed on Calvary Jesus is exciting as Call of duty or Harry Potter Hell couldn't get any hotter Foxe Book of the martyrs Mission Impossible My Redeemer Lives The Ultimate sacrifice is that He Gives ...David slew Goliath with one smooth stone I can make a call to heaven without a cellular digital phone

You want to have a conversation with spiritual being's nothings more freeing than have the devil fleeing. Hearing God and seeing the mission impossible manifest like healing or better yet salvation Yahshua Ha Mashiach to the nations this is for OUR Generation Salvation By Joseph Taliaferro aka Brother P

Minister Farrakhan meets Brother P Dream

Me and Minister Louis Farrakhan met in a dream. I was riding past his building, inside of the building was a big meeting room and he had a lot of guys around him. I could see this from outside of the Building. As I was passing by the next thing was I was in the building but this time there was no security with him it was just me and the Minister. He walked up to me and started talking to me about Jesus. After listening for a while I said that Jesus Hebrew name was Yahshua. He did not respond and immediately turned around and walked away from me.

The next thing you know I was out in a van like truck pulling off. As I drove away one of the security guys was running after the truck trying to get the license plate number, but it wasn't like i was trying to get away. I just went around the side of the building in the truck but the thing about it is the truck hit the side of the building that they were in which alerted them to come after me. I drove around the corner where there was another abandoned building.

I went to check it out and suddenly it turned into a church. A couple of ministers popped up I asked them what's going on in the building, they said that the people just got evicted for not paying the rent. I asked how much was the rent and the ministers said don't worry about it we'll work it out. The next scene I'm in a church and I'm sitting beside my wife. These things were like back to back and she has a little baby in her hands and my cousin sits beside her and boom he has a little baby in his hands also. So now it's these two babies that are wrapped up.

At the time my wife was pregnant, and I wanted a little boy but in the dream, she was holding a baby girl. I knew then I was having a girl and that other little baby boy ....

well 2 years later that baby boy was born.

To all those who are followers of the Honorable Elijah Muhammad and Minister Louis Farrakhan there is a Savior. Minister Farrakhan and other NOI Minister state that Elijah Muhammed is Jesus of the new Testament and They have Master Fard Muhammad as the messiah according to the final call, but the Savior of the world is Yahshua Ha Mashiach according to the scriptures. He was born of the virgin Mary, shed his blood on Golgotha for our sins and rose from the dead and sent his spirit back. The Ruach ha Kodesh on Pentecost day over 2,000 years ago. People maybe able to save you from this or that But Yahshua/Jesus Christ is the only Savior that can snatch you out of the Kingdom of satan into the Kingdom of YHVH.

For God so loved the world, that he gave his only begotten Son, that whosoever believeth in him should not perish, but have everlasting life.   John 3 :16

After my Nation of Islam experience, I began studying the teaching of Dr. Malachi Z. York. After becoming a follower of Yahshua and reading the bible for myself could clearly see that the priesthood in the Nuwaubian organization was not the priesthood according to the Book of Hebrews in the New Testament.

⁶ I marvel that ye are so soon removed from him that called you into the grace of Christ unto another gospel:
⁷ Which is not another; but there be some that trouble you, and would pervert the gospel of Christ.
⁸ But though we, or an angel from heaven, preach any other gospel unto you than that which we have preached unto you, let him be accursed.
⁹ As we said before, so say I now again, if any man preach any other gospel unto you than that ye have received, let him be accursed.
¹⁰ For do I now persuade men, or God? or do I seek to please men? for if I yet pleased men, I should not be the servant of Christ. Galatian 1

Dr. York Dream

I was in a mall and I was with my fraternity brothers. A young lady came up and stole my wallet while we sat at a table. The brothers wanted to help me get my wallet back but in a flash, they were all outside of the building in a car. This car was locked up to the point that they could not get out of it to help me.

As I look for this young lady in this mall I turn a corner and I am suddenly in a food court. I walked into and open restaurant and walk up to the counter and now me and Dr. York are face to face. We did not say anything to each other and then he was gone. I went to the back of his restaurant and noticed his Portrait was hanging on the wall. I grabbed it with both hands and pulled it down and as I came up with my hands I had a picture of Yahshua and I put it on the walk in the same place. Then I went to the front where an alter was located. On the alter was a copy of the Holy Tablets. A book written by Dr. York that contained most of the scrolls that Dr. York had written over the years. While looking at the alter the whole thing went down into the ground and when it came back up a Bible was on the alter replacing The Holy Tablets …**Then I woke Up.**

Through the Nuwaubians I learned about Melchizadek. Dr. York basically was making the claim that he was Melchizadek . Melchizadek is the King of Righteousness according to the Bible in the book of Hebrews. The revelation I received in the written word is that Yahshua is the fulfillment of the Title. Saints and future saints Yahshua/Jesus Christ is the King of Kings and when you enter his rest. You will enter The Royal Priesthood of Melchizadek

Moonwalking

Man, ain't never been on the Moon and we did not evolve from Baboons

There's a star that can save your soul and then there's that star over the North Pole

The heavens declare His glory watch the stars revolve and tell a story

the skies proclaim the work of his hands The World awaits the Return of the Son of Man

Polaris is the Center all-stars revolve The Earth is still The Aleph and Tav weave and Bob satan hand is on the door knob

brainwash the babies in science class mention Yah's creation and you might not pass how long will this tomfoolery last

the earth is not spinning earthling are sinning Copernicus lies and social darwinning the minds of the youth, But the Truth is Yah wake up from the spell of amen ra honor your pa and ma and research the north star it's all in the

scriptures you must be born again let the spirit hit ya The Blood of the Lamb is what covers the sin now let's begin.

you want see p moonwalk on stage we in the grip of the New age as the awe and rumors of war rage The Beast is about to be released from his cage to take his seat in the third and claim he God

read Thessalonians and see it yourself become Revelation and help someone else without the seal of yah you going to take that Mark the enemy will bite without you hearing his Bark but he not that smart he let the Cross go down Now the Lamb is Coming Back as a Lion wearing a crown

Houston, we got a problem and that problem is the bible. I moved to Houston Texas in early 2016. My first Job was as a security guard at a construction site. 48 hours a week for 6 months I watched the sun and moon travel across the sky, My Job was to sit in my Van and observe the traffic going in and out of the site. In a 12 hour shift I was able to see the sun make roughly the same path every day. This made me think because as a science student I was taught that the earth was revolving and spinning around the sun. My thoughts were if this was true then there should be a drastic change in the position of the sun after a 6-month period. No change was visible. This drove me back to the book of Genesis. I dug into chapter 1 like an archeologist. The first thing that I noticed was that the Heaven and the Earth were created on the first day of Creation. The Sun Moon and Stars were created on the Forth day. Hold Up …Houston We got A Problem!

I thought the statement Let There Be Light was about the Sun, but it was about the Son of the Living God. Yahshua is The Light of the World. And if you go to Rev 21 you will see that The New Jerusalem Will have no need for the Sun and Moon because the Glory of Yahshua will be The Light.

Then spake Jesus again unto them, saying, I am the light of the world: he that followeth me shall not walk in darkness, but shall have the light of life. John 8

Ye are the light of the world. A city that is set on a hill cannot be hid. Neither do men light a candle, and put it under a bushel, but on a candlestick; and it giveth light unto all that are in the house. Let your light so shine before men, that they may see your good works, and glorify you father which is in Heaven, Matthew 5

I graduated from college with a degree in Building Construction Technology in 1989. I worked on a Survey crew for two years. I started as a chainman /rodman then 4 months later I became the instrument man for the City of Riverside Ca.

The scriptures in the bible did not line up with Copernicus heliocentric theory. THEORY is the problem just like the theory of evolution these theories have become the truth and the scriptures have been rejected and kicked out of state education.

First of all, the Bible speaks of a dome above us. And waters above the Dome. The Sun Moon and Stars are all below this dome. The North Star, Polaris is directly above the North Pole. This star does not move and through photography you can observe in a 24-hour period all the stars revolve around this one star like a big old Clock. Now we can go back to my dream of the Stars falling into formation to form the Son of Man Yahshua. What were those stars in my dream. They were the Angels that serve YHVH. Yahshua is the bright and morning Star and His angels are the Host of heaven.

As I `continued to dig into the scriptures I came to Genesis 6 where the Sons of God took the daughters of men for wives. Their children were called the Nephilim. After Noah's flood these being were destroyed but those spirits did not drown they are the demons that we have even unto this day. Another source of Knowledge is the Book of Enoch. Many will not read this book because they have been brainwashed into thinking the bible only consist of 66 books. This is not true, The Ethiopian cannon has about 81 books that include the apocrypha The Book of Enock and The Book of Jubilees.

I read the Book of Enoch translated by R H Charles while working overnight in a Jail. After reading every word. I read it again with a Highlighter. There was not one contradiction with my King James Version of the bible. This book not only breaks down angels and the fallen angels, but it clearly gives exact knowledge about the paths of the Sun and Moon. This is a section of our 66-book bible.

14 And Enoch also, the seventh from Adam, prophesied of these, saying, Behold, the Lord cometh with ten thousands of his saints,

15 To execute judgment upon all, and to convince all that are ungodly among them of all their ungodly deeds which they have ungodly committed, and of all their hard speeches which ungodly sinners have spoken against him.

The Book of Jude

So yes, I believe that the earth is not spinning and revolving around the sun. The Creation is not aimlessly flinging through space. So, Men have walked on the moon from 1968 to 1972? If we did go to the moon with that primitive technology Great. 50 years Later let us go back. There is no excuse why America has not put mankind on the Moon during the mid-70's, 80's, 90's, 00's ,10's. The Only reason we have not gone back to the Moon is we never went. Prove me wrong NASA not with words but with Deeds. Forget Mars Let Go Back to the MOON.

Yes, the Bible is a science and a history book. Books like Maccabees are world history. In America we have separation of church and state what does that have to do with truth and facts. Powers to be don't want The Whole Truth and nothing but the Truth.

How could satanist and witches be covered by freedom of religion. How could demonic racist continue to claim a connection to Jesus. But one sweet Day Truth is coming back to completely set the record straight. Until then we the ambassadors will continue to spread the good news and speak Truth to power. Yahshua /Jesus is The Truth

Lakewood church

Upon arriving in Houston, we attended Lakewood church on several occasions. The first time we came to Lakewood and older white gentleman met me in the lobby. We talked for several minutes and I shared with him that I needed a 4-bedroom house. He told me that his mother in law had a house for rent. I was like wow we just moved here and just like that we found a home. The next week I met with his mother in law. She was an older Mexican lady and spoke very little English. But everything was cool and after meeting twice she decided to rent the house to us. Friday came, and we checked out of the hotel. She finally called me and informed that I was going to have to wait another week. After I got off the phone I found a weekly hotel for my family. After a month or so I decided to concentrate on my job and forget about this house.....

Crazy Dream

This dream takes place in a house. Me and an older white man was having a conversation and he did not noticed that I slipped into his garage where There was a young Hispanic lady waiting patiently waiting in the driver seat. She did not hear or see me as I looked into the back seat I saw all kinds of instruments in the back seat to cut me up. I slipped back into the house and the gentlemen was preparing drinks for us. He put something in one of the cups to put me OUT. He sat the drinks down and when he turned his back I switch the drinks. We drank and that was the end of that dream.

The Older gentleman called me a couple week later and ask me if I wanted to use his clothing voucher for free clothes at the thrift store. I asked him why did he have a voucher. He informed me that His house had been destroyed in a fire. I was like wow.

During this time, we had written a Letter to Lakewood church for housing assistance. We had money but renting a house was tough because we were new to Houston. Lakewood sent us a letter that they could not help us, and they would be praying for us.

We stayed in the hotel for three months and finally a large apartment became available with a month rent free. 15 months later a large house opened for us. A day before we had to renew our apartment lease.

After moving into the apartment, the older lady called me and asked me if I still wanted to rent her house. I said No Thank You.

I am a preacher and I became one 16 years ago when I was snatched out of the Kingdom of satan into the Kingdom of YHVH. I was ordained by Yah to preach the good news. Many who are teaching, and preaching use the name Hebrew Israelites. I have found that like many churches the Hebrew community has many camps. That range from hardcore young men and women that reject the virgin birth to camps that believe in the operation of the gifts of the Spirit. Who side am I on? None of them I Love Yahshua!

Whites and blacks are in a total state of confusion. Because the trap was set many moons ago when men decide to classify people according to appearance. Now we have a group called the whites and a group called the blacks. White Jews and Black Jews all need to be born again and filled with the holy spirit. Some black Hebrew Israelites point to the scriptures about the synagogue of satan. And based on the assumption that some white Jews are converts they talk as if they all are converts. The Question should be are there any Jews other than the so called white Jews in Modern Day Israel. The Answer is yes. So regardless of the Politics, religious fighting and debating. Those who are claiming that they are Israel are headed to the land from all over the world.

The synagogue of satan is bigger than so called fake Jews. Just Like the body of Christ are all who are filled with the Spirit of YHVH in the name of Yahshua . The Synagogue of satan or the body of the anti-christ is all those who are filled with the spirit of satan. An One day the powers to be in that nation are going to build the Third Temple. When this happens the scripture states that the man of sin will exalt himself and sit as god in the Temple. And when this happens YHVH will destroy him and everybody who did not receive the love of the truth that they might be saved. *2 Thessalonians 2*

If a man/woman is leading a group of people and they begin to worship that person. What spirit is in that man if he does not correct those followers. Classic cults are groups of people that worship their human leader. Worship is an act that is meant for God and God alone. Who is your God? Yahshua accepted worship because he is Immanuel.

Matthew 14:33 — Then those who were in the boat came and worshiped Him, saying, "Truly You are the Son of God."

Matthew 28:17 — When they saw Him, they worshiped Him; but some doubted

John 5:23 — *that all should honor the Son just as they honor the Father. He who does not honor the Son does not honor the Father who sent Him."*

John 9:38 — *Then he said, "Lord, I believe!" And he worshiped Him.*

Hebrews 1:6 — *But when He again brings the firstborn into the world, He says: "Let all the angels of God worship Him*

Jay Z Dream This next rhyme comes out of a dream I had several years ago. I saw the face of Jay Z, Nas and R Kelly and then a tombstone pops up with the word witchcraft on it. And that is what sparked the idea to write this song using the Harry Potter book titles as my paint

Harry Potter Christians

In a dream I saw the word witchcraft along with Jay Z, Nas and R Kelly....my favorite movie was belly deals are made artist doing the harry potter, partners get played .... building on philosopher's stones never prayed, got many men talking to snakes all gas no brakes.... revealing a chamber of secrets mythologies seducing spirits and doctrines of the fallen ones, these days Christians are strapped they carry guns as if bullets can protect against the spiritual, they posted up in them chambers performing rituals this demonic power is habitual ......a prisoner escaped from Azkaban a mass murderer hollering yes we can my kids eat peanut butter but avoid peter pan taking yours to a fantasy rat land, for the saints it's not wise we up against so many third eyes surprise tasting the strange wine served in goblets of Fire saving souls is Pees only desire.... Jehovah witnesses a new world order of the phoenix bird crash and burn to rise up again with the power of death the wages of sin, the plot is thick satan will

take your breath use you like a slave till there no use left
…. the half-blood prince is not the prince of peace out of
the deathly hallows comes forth from the east after 1000
years the lake of fire will welcome the beast and only then
will the wars cease, the church needs to wake up and enjoy
the feast of Yahweh harry potter fan gets saved burns the
books today was a good day, I made you look your shook
we were not given a spirit of Fear to those who have ears
let them hear

One World Religion

One world religion kiss the ring of your leaders death is
the fate of so called useless feeders population control
abortion and diseases for the breeders psalms 91 the secret
place to hide believers concentration camps after they
confiscate the heaters….no beats by Dre no Nikes Rev
Run in My Adidas I met The King of Kings in Jamaica
Queens everything ain't what it seems High Beams
…..Pigs alligators crows doves and a pigeon new world
order the one world religion aint nothing new under the
sun contracts are being laid out angels of light come in the
name of fun ….

They'll take you to the top of the temple and show you
how the world could be yours simple but hold up wait the
small print has some crazy stipulations will I be able to
rock at these congregations? Yes…. just bow down in
secrecy the world will love you and not even know that
you are following the enemy of all Mankind crack open
the book and read between the lines the signs the wonders
the Lightning the thunder The Blood of Jesus Christ will
break the spell that You are Under….Wake Up churches
synagogues and mosque are openly new age as if faith is
faith the combination of religion and state it's all in Ezekiel

8 as we hand out wedding invitations no one knows the date a prophecy about the sun worshippers weeping for tammuz you want to preach the good news you will pay your dues...

The Word is powerful I love the red letters. the voice of God and no one does it better like Etta James ...…I want a Sunday kind of love from up above descending back down like a dove no push no shove…. Respect the process embrace the transition learning how to listen before

rejecting dismissing, cuz at the end of the day everyman can walk in error in the name of Jesus I don't want to be a terror to those who are seeking just as I was way back then found a friend who gave me power over my sin that i was born in now IM born again drink this water its spiritual

Brother P is Lyrical knowing it'll take a miracle... Yes, a virgin gave birth to save the earth through his shed blood the Passover lamb is love the true manna the bread of life the bride of Christ a biblical example of a man being a wife 10 virgins check the sample be wise.

Sick and tired of being sick and tired you fired a state of poverty is no longer admired prosperity been hired provision from heaven has been wired the advisory is a liar now sit back and enjoy my choir …we out never to return to this lower level lucifer satan the beast it all equal to the devil three degree no shovel death burial resurrection perverted an anointed cherub into a rebel my rock is flawless diamond embezzled hit the gas pedal i was raised hip hop and was influenced by heavy metal no compromising on the word i will not settle blood and flesh p will try not to wrestle... lawless rebellious thinking while the world is on the brinkin eyes wide shut but you can smell the garbage is stinking what wrong with your

left eye its blinking i saw you hoodwinking in flint
Michigan lead water is what they drinking what really
happened to president Abraham Lincoln run for the hills
no more tattoo on the body of the messiah even though the
mark is not inking …no you do not have my permission to
kill me i died 15 years ago the real ones all feel me take a
trip to negroland to destroy and steal me the blood spilled
to heal me. no need for stigmata here comes the lion from
the tribe of Judah the streets will always respect the
shooter when spiritual plumbing need assistances call the
only divine roto rooter he helps remove waste products
urine and manure salt water is the cure …angels coming
with sickles straight swinging them things anointed vessels
smoking sticky green caught up in street gangs touch there
god if you want to see fangs hate will make the
thingamajigga bang my savior committed no sin but it was
written he would hang from a tree born black in America it
has got to be a curse before you debate with brother p read
Deuteronomy first …cursed is any man that hangeth on
tree it is written propaganda got you believing that an
apple was bitten Michelangelo and Davinci was tripping
Christ has redeemed from the curse of the law that's
redemption I almost forgot to mention …Jesus is black
now tell me how did that make you feel it just got real
…Jesus is white now tell me how did that make you feel it
just got real …maybe he is Russian a Viking or
Vietnamese think about it He is a Hebrew Israelite Negro
Please love yourself and if yah is in you I'll meet you in
the new Jerusalem at the Venue …breath on them dry
bones Lazarus come forth and take them grave clothes east
to west south to the north written he would hang from a
tree born black in America it has got to be a curse before
you debate with brother p read Deuteronomy first

Brace Yourself When a driver foresees an upcoming bump along the road, he/she usually warns his/her passengers by asking them to brace themselves: I hear the spirit of the Lord saying, "Brace yourself, you'll come against some challenges, you'll experience some difficulties but brace yourself, don't be alarmed, don't look at the rearview mirror, but ...hold on to me,
I got the wheel."

YHVH was with Me the Whole Time!

The year was around 1998.and I had moved to Atlanta Ga. I worked at The Hilton Hotel downtown. One evening we started talking about Liquor and they were saying that tequila was a crazy drink. I just listened and was thinking tequila is no different than any other liquor. My partner from Carolina had told me about Club 559 and I decided to check it out. I went straight to bar and ordered a couple of beers and a shot of the tequila. Okay then I ordered another shot classic tequila with the lime and salt. Now a few minutes later I felt the initial effect of the Tefilla shots. I then saw a frat brother come in the Club. I demanded that he take a shot with me. He resisted and then gave in to the bruh pressure. Several brews and the third shot down was a GO.

I was officially LIT. I rarely would be dancing at this stage in my life. But there I was in the middle of the dance floor, getting all the way down. There were girls all around me and I was not even there. I could see myself dancing. Yes, I was out of my body watching Me dance. Then after what I thought was a lifetime The DJ stopped the music and I froze. My spirit and flesh were reunited. I was done. I made my way back to the bar. I grab the bar to gather myself and prepare mentally to drive home. Yes, I was prepared to drive home drunk. And out of nowhere my

Frat brother is in my face with another shot of Tequila. I tried to say no, but he used the same Bruh tactics on me that I used on Him.

The shot went down in slow motion. When it hit rock bottom I blacked out. My next memory is at the door of the Club. I blacked out and came to at the door of my car. I blacked out and then I came to inside the car putting the key in the ignition and after it started I blacked out.
I came to on the Highway to Smyrna Ga. Travelling around 60 miles per hour. I went right back unconscious behind the will and came to at my apartment.
My roommate Llewelyn Radford was sleep but he kept the apartment freezing cold. I fell asleep with sweaty wet clothes on and woke up sick as a dog. Jesus took the wheel that night.

Calling

What have I gotten myself into
I do love you but to myself I must remain true
I'm not refusing you I'm not abusing you
 if I'm confusing you I feel I'm losing you
 I wonder why I do all of the things I do
someone is calling me and it is not you
 I can hear my name this voice is not the same he told me
stop playing around this is not a game
I woke up early in the morning and began to weep still
dark outside my flesh is still asleep. through dreams and
vision, he began to speak I am said launch out into the
deep, my light will be a path unto your feet new wine is
the drink my bread you'll eat
submit to my will and I will show you the way fellowship
meditate and never cease to pray
Perfection yes saints we can get love your enemies no way

we can forget that good Samaritans that's a commandment faith comes by a preacher that heaven sent… never bent or caught up in filthy lucre you saved good someone can still shoot ya, so stay ready because it's all about to manifest Shabbat Shalom right to left that's peace and rest no stress just lift the savior up

Who am I just a soldier laying in the psalms 91 Matthew 24 cut what's up

The Beast Vision

After study reading about the end times I knew some of the signs of the emergence of the anti-Christ. This event would proceed the second coming of Jesus Christ according to the scriptures. And even though I had a grasp of the anti-Christ spirit that was already in the world 2000 years ago, I did not have a clue who this person was.

Then I had a vision of Prince Charles I saw his face very clearly. And then his head did a 180-degree turn. The image was a Hideous Beast.I never even thought of looking at the royal family in connection to end time prophecy. One day a Brother in Christ heard my dream and said he saw Prince William as the Beast.

Most people think of the royals in England as just figure heads. But with a little digging I realized that The Queen oversees that country.

I went to a bible study in Savannah Ga and Pastor Chip Brown's topic was Revelation 13. And that's when I saw something very interesting.

[11] And I beheld another beast coming up out of the earth; and he had two horns like a lamb, and he spake as a dragon.[12] And he exerciseth all the power of the first beast before him, and causeth the earth and them which dwell therein to worship the first beast, whose deadly wound was healed. Revelation 13

Two Beast in the Book of Revelation. My thoughts that evening were a father and son situation. Well because of my dream I had confidence in rejecting Bush, Obama and Trump as the anti-Christ. I am of the strong opinion that the beast will have a worldly blood line that makes a claim of royalty and privilege to rule the world.

Pimp Shoe Dream

I came across a security deposit box unit outside. I resemble the Mailboxes at an apart complex. The type where the mail man could deliver the Mail to everybody at one location instead of going door to door.
As I approached the boxes as noticed that all of the doors were open. In each security box was a pair of expensive alligator skin shoes. Inside of each shoe were to jewels. Well I reach in a box and grabbed a pair of the precious jewels from out of the shoe and put them in my pocket.
As soon as I put the jewels in my pocket a security guard was alerted and bean coming towards me. I began walking away from not wanting to get caught. While I was walking a smoothly dropped the jewels out of my pocket one at a time on to the ground. After the second jewel was out of my possession the security guard grabbed me.

Molested
If I could change the world
and make it a better place
and put a smile on every child's face
the shame the hurt the pain
molested by a world insane
I see your true colors
True colors are beautiful
Like a rainbow
innocence lost all trust gone what kind of love is this what
kind of love would hurt a loved one ...no protection babies

are in danger people in pain cause pain and that is no
excuse when it rains it pours virgin bodies broken by lust
.... enough to make a preacher cuss happiness is left in the
dust but God can heal a broken heart and turn ashes into
beauty ...
it's beautiful when you hear testimonies of deliverance and
salvation to this adulterous generation there is hope for
abusers and victims of abuse .... loose them in the name of
Yahshua and bind up every foul and unclean spirit in Jesus
Name I proclaim victory and liberty in the presence of love
real love agape love

Seduced

I am looking at you and I see a woman on the screen and
stage but you a man is this an act are you acting or acting

out due to the hurt that was given by someone who
probably was hurt the same way. Man, this is crazy the
effect that you can have in someone's life ...who would
ever hurt a child or worse a baby how a man becomes a
lady I cannot believe it's all sexual it has to be mental
psychological and definitely spiritual.

 seduced by a monster an angel of light a wolf in sheep's
clothing predators are roaming it's not safe anymore or was
it ever really safe since the serpent is subtle and crafty
sneaky shifty and manipulative

real love will give a second chance the holy spirit will
enhance every kiss and every dance between two that were
divinely put together so why take his name in vain got the
masses saying halayluyer no its halleluYah shua is the Key
and the door... The transformation of a sinner Marriage is
honorable in all, and the bed undefiled: but whoremongers
and adulterers God will judge

Who is the Star

Is the Great cloud of Witnesses separated into clicks? Carnal congregations have so many tricks on earth as it is in Heaven .... Selah Seven. The Prince of Peace is the King

of Salem eliminating leaven...The remnant is waking up Yahshua's the Star Come out come out come out wherever you are...Church splits and beef like those preachers' Biggie and Pac Soon ushers will welcome you in with their hand on their gloc tic toc funeral services in the church building Who decided to bring dead bodies amongst Yah's children? I'm free I'm free claiming the Victory.... In Yahshua not over Yah's people the so-called Laity...Who are all priest ...royal ...the hood is loyal Leviathan must be cast out or that snake will coil like a boa constrictor squeezing and choking Pokémon poking weeding and coking don't think

I'm smoking I'm not joking but what's provoking the real saints to start walking...Mr. .... you been preaching for a long time ... Talking and talking. The streets is watching checking your lifestyle for humility and meekness

But all they see is the pride. The enemy knows your weakness. But we know his ....and it's the Blood of the Passover Lamb Yahshua Ha Mashiach Ruach ha Kodesh the Great I AM.

What if people flat out stop going to CHURCH? A whole bunch of Pastors would be flat out of Work... Monday morning Lord now you got to get a Job Offering plate Mafia taught you how to rob.

Brainwash, Mind control primping Them tricks. Got the body of Jesus Christ Rolling in CLICKS...

Baptist, Methodist COGIC whoopty whoop the top of the pyramid not really part of the group.

The heads connect politic at the Players Ball... When them demons start manifesting who are you going to call. Pastor this and Pa Pa Pastor that Pastor at the mall fresh Gators and the matching Hat. So before you rebuke remember I

AM free Go Holla at your Pimp and tell Him or Her to holla at Me.

American as Apple Pie

The Blood of Yahshua was shed for even enemies of the cross the chief cornerstone that the builders rejected is for the lost no need to cut chicken heads off or fly around like Harry potter your rap skills are tight ...you wannabee Sean Carter... He also be trying to kill Jesus, but you know he already died. the Resurrection of the Messiah is death to a foolish man's PRIDE ...Plucks out your third eye now your two eyes that were created by My YAH begin to CRY the

realization of the lie Snake cults are as American as apple pie

Can you hear shofar blowing walls breaking infrastructures crashing demon spirits dashing as I unleash this beautiful lashing So while you ride goats backwards I will continue to warn the sheep and remember when casting spells you can sow but be prepared to reap...

Why not reap love In Yahshua You can REST this life that you Are living in reality is JUST A TEST

Your failing the test but homie but it's never too late you want it right now but with Yahshua you going to have to wait. no patience ...but life will teach some vital lessons, vital signs, flat lines, every now and then bring precious blessings no need for guessing

I'm not your enemy you made of flesh but them spirit guides you are chilling with get no rest, yes it's the Blood of The Passover Lamb that frees, I shoot the breeze, under Carolina palm trees 95 17 come across da traxxx when them lights go out it ain't nothing but blacks,

root workers, crack smokers, and some of them is preachers ..it's going to take a real miracle to reach ya but LOVE gone teach ya ..Those demons will only beat ya like your big brother from back in the daze who was glad to meet ya…

Meet the Greeks who at first was your best friend until you went online and caught that paddle and cane again and again ...an evil grin is the grill that the made ones make as they death march to a memorial service after a wake. Wake up Wake up some bodies calling your name.......

Brand New

Some say I shouldn't chop it up with a brother who practices voodoo but who are you? And are you honest about what you do?

See p is a brand-new creature but I remember back in the dayz when I was caught up in a purple haze 6 million wayz Before the gospel music the gospel plays some thought it was just a phase…

Then the wife came the 9 babies 4 little fellas and 5 little ladies, the tears flow it just amazes me it's crazy who knows I know my Yah can speak through Beyoncé and really get at Jay Z …Don't praise me when I flow this thang I just can't let go it got me for real broken hearts can heal Isaiah 58 the hungry need a meal the thirsty just need a drink stop listen and think the world is on the brink of world war 3 disaster after disaster but theirs Rest in the Master no need to worship your pastor …

Don't you know who you Are? You are the light of the World with the Bright and Morning Star Yahshua in the center knocking at the Door of your heart offering a brand-new start waiting for you to answer so He can enter.

He will take your burdens I mean all who are heavy laden and now I am really fading so My Yahshua can increase we are the body of the Prince of Peace. The Body of the Messiah Let his love take you Higher and higher now that's Fire Water Living Water Brother Phil is not for hire the hireling will cause the sheep to scatter no foolish chit chatter the uncompromising word is the real crux of the matter....

Don't Cheat
Fellas don't cheat on them remember never ever beat on them you better not sleep on them it will never be the same if you creep on them ..Don't listen my brother I'll see you in jail waiting on your folks to post the bail tears of pain while you in that cell a women can make your life heaven or hell … I'm doing this song cuz I had a dream you thought you was slick cuz you had a scheme
That grass on the other side is a shade of green that sweet little girl you gone make her mean …
What Yah puts together won't be coming apart. let this word sink in and guard your heart ...love is not a game and war is not an art end foolishness before it can start ONE
Smokers
All of my dreams and desires seems like they were going up in fire Yahshua a came in and started a blaze now my soul is going higher and higher in Yah ….I got a one step program if you want to quit never in your life will you take another hit ….marijuana youngins call it Loud fire in your brains satan turning you Out…I got that Living water some call it H20 separate the atoms and watch the elements

Blow smoking sticky green leaves with my kinfolk smoke to you choke smoke to you broke…I'm in the vill with the hustlers and dope dealers outback steakhouse blokes and the Sheila's gun drama bullets pop jail and body bags I move fast I'm in the bottom buying dime bags …I never thought I would end up a dope fiend but it is what it is and it's not a dream it's a nightmare now I got a hangover praying to a porcelain god it can't get any lower the next day a voice told me not to eat meat I obeyed no more burger king or mickey dees… Eating salads and still on that ganja smoke called a shorty from the yard who loved the dope she didn't come so I smoke the blunt solo fell asleep woke up and here we go …Super natural Light shining straight through my ceiling I felt like a vampire I really can't describe the feeling but I know that the taste for weed was no longer in me I was free His name is Victory… 15 years of burning up my brain cells took a toll I would freeze up go blank ice cold My soul in one day was restored can't you hear the son of God knocking at your Door... call the Dr. his name is mercy and Grace hear his voice and seek His Face Jesus

When a person makes a deal with the enemy, when they choose to do his bidding, he uses them to the utmost, the heart becomes as cold as stone & they are enticed to a game where every trick is permissible: betrayal, backstabbing, cheating…anything to get the job done but He also exposes their character in the process: Judas didn't only have to sell Jesus to the Roman soldiers, but he also had to seal the deal w/ a KISS!

The Serpent Beguiled Eve in the Garden of Eden... In today's day and age, if a serpent ever speaks to a Believer or ever tries to come near them, he or she would run for dear life but BEWARE of the Sly Fox, the Wolf in Sheep's Clothing...WEAR the Full Armor of God at all times!

He left the family nest and ventured in the world, to live "La Vida Loca" but his dreams soon vanished and he was confronted with a harsh reality... so broke, disgusted, disillusioned ..with friends and fortune gone, his eyes were finally opened to the fact that there was only One PERSON who would still give him a second chance ~ as far as the east is from the west, so far has he removed our transgressions from us !

I must renew my Mind(rhyme)

...This is My Last Time ...I know you want to worry about me but I'm going to be fine, I saw a sign Light gave me Bread and Wine. What I received in my Spirit is One of a Kind, Yahshua came in

and delivered Me then I began to Breath He Put his Word In My Heart Then I Began to read, I found out who He was and That He Came to Save My Soul He is The Greatest of All Time His Is The Greatest Story ever Told.Yahshua

"That Hebrew slave you've had around here tried to make a fool of me,"(she could probably win an Oscar for her acting skills.) and as a result of that, Joseph was imprisoned, but don't be distraught over that, because NO WEAPON FORMED AGAINST GOD'S CHILDREN SHALL PROSPER ~ Don't try to COMPROMISE in order to stay in a place that the the Lord has already released you from, TRUST that HE is taking you HIGHER!
Markeda Taliaferro

A Divine Visitation

While standing in a beautiful field I saw a Man and he was looking at me with no expression on his face. After a few moments I knew that this was Yahshua, the son of the living God. I asked him to give me a gift and he turned and began to walk away. I said you ascended unto heaven and left gifts unto men. After hearing this he stopped in his tracks and turned around and faced me. I was no longer standing in the field by myself a close ministry partner was standing next to me in the field. Yahshua instructed both of us to turn our heads because what he was about to do we would not be able to visually handle.

I saw him raise up his hands and his hands as they became balls of fire. And then flames came out of both hands like laser beams and hit me and my ministry partner in the chest. After the fire was inside of us Yahshua and my ministry partner was gone, and I was standing in the field with a shofar in my hand. I took the shofar and began to blow into the sky everywhere I pointed the shofar the clouds would disperse, I was amazed at the power of the shofar to move the clouds with sound.

At that very moment I was translated out of the field into the streets of New York City. I noticed many orthodox Jews in their traditional black garbs walking around. I felt that this was the perfect time to use my new gift to bring these orthodox Jews into the knowledge of the messiah that they rejected for so many years. As I began to blow the shofar I quickly realized that I could barely make a sound. They noticed me struggling with the shofar and continued doing what they were doing. I was distraught at this point I was translated back to the beautiful field. Where Yahshua and my ministry partner were standing.

Yahshua told me that my gift worked with my ministry partner's gift.

My Travel through fraternities, religions, jobs, entertainment, social networks and academic institutions have been interesting to say the least. Anything can be classified as a cult. Depending on who you ask to define a cult will determine the definition. So, I would rather concentrate on a relationship with the Creator.

My Relationship with Yahshua whom all things were created through has led and guided my path. And because I know his voice I know when he is leading me. Before I turned from my wicked ways I was being tossed backward and forward by charismatic leaders and doctrines of devils. But all that ended when Yah sealed me with his Holy Spirit and I will end this book with the solution to LIES.

If ye love me, keep my commandments. And I will pray the Father, and he shall give you another Comforter, that he may abide with you forever; Even the Spirit of truth; whom the world cannot receive, because it seeth him not, neither knoweth him: but ye know him; for he dwelleth with you, and shall be in you. I will not leave you comfortless: I will come to you. Yet a little while, and the world seeth me no more; but ye see me: because I live, ye shall live also. At that day ye shall know that I am in my Father, and ye in me, and I in you. John 14

Did I Just Join a Cult? is the Question and the answer is yes. I was born into a cult called America. Cults are as American as apple pie. Because our country turned the founders of the United States into gods. They worship documents like the constitution as if it is scripture. American Culture worships people and turns them into idols. This is a condition that has led to a reprobate state .

Who changed the truth of God into a lie, and worshipped and served the creature more than the Creator, who is blessed forever. Amen.

26 For this cause God gave them up unto vile affections: for even their women did change the natural use into that which is against nature:

27 And likewise also the men, leaving the natural use of the woman, burned in their lust one toward another; men with men working that which is unseemly, and receiving in themselves that recompence of their error which was meet.

28 And even as they did not like to retain God in their knowledge, God gave them over to a reprobate mind, to do those things which are not convenient;

Romans 1

Is there Hope? Yes. America as a country must repent for breeding a culture of hate, greed, lust, murder, perversion and everything else that is contrary to the Word of Yah through a change of laws, statutes and policies for YHVH to heal Our Country's Broken heart. But please don't wait for the country or your city to change, let us examine ourselves and allow the Holy Spirit to transform us into the Lights of this World as we wait for the Light of the World to return. Yahshua is The King of Kings.

2 Chronicles 7:14
14 If my people, which are called by my name, shall humble themselves, and pray, and seek my face, and turn from their wicked ways; then will I hear from heaven, and will forgive their sin, and will heal their land.

Jesus is a Black Man. I mean since it doesn't matter what color he is. Jesus is God ... So, Yea God is a Black man...They made all the race color stuff up and it is the basis for social Darwinism and eugenics (Murder out of lies and Hate). So, let's roll with it if we accept this fake color is a race dynamic. Let's define a member of the Black race ..one drop rule foolishness resulted in the black race looking like every ethnic group and nationality...Caucasoid Mongoloid and Negroid Black people (one drop rule /law)

Let's define a member of the white race .... they must look white and therefore you have millions of so called blacks passing as white and you will never know until you test for sickle cell. or if you shake the family tree and boom a negro plum falls off.

scripture time....
But the Lord said unto Samuel, "Look not on his countenance or on the height of his stature, because I have refused him; for the Lord seeth not as man seeth. For man looketh on the outward appearance, but the Lord looketh on the heart." 1 SAMUEL 16:7

To the Saints and Future Saints: YHVH is your Heavenly Father, Yahshua is your Savior , Noah is your Biological Great Grand Daddy therefore Family . Brother P will see you at the Family Reunion in The New Jerusalem. Shalom

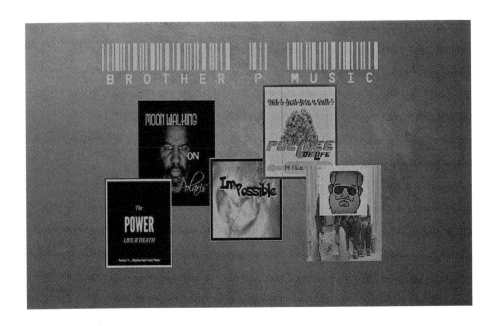

Book Brother P (Joseph Taliaferro) for ministry and speaking engagements

uberbrotherp@gmail.com or call @ 3462270886

Stream for free if you like download for a fee

http://uberbrotherp.com/brother_p_music__5_cd_s/

These 5 Cd's are the soundtrack for the Book
The Link above is my website
www.uberbrotherp.com   You may also find
the Music at CD Baby
**https://store.cdbaby.com/Artist/Brother
P**
Thank You for your support and if you would
like to donate to this ministry you can become
a Patron at
https://www.patreon.com/uberbrotherp or
donate through paypal paypal.me/TheWell
Testimony Blog exbglounion.wordpress.com

Made in the USA
Columbia, SC
26 January 2022